Dimension 2008

Languages for the Nation

Dennis R. Miller, Jr.
David Alley
Denise Overfield
Edwina Spodark
Patricia Early
Peter B. Swanson
Marat Sanatullov
Rosalie Cheatham
Elvira Sanatullova-Allison
Lisa F. Signori

Editors
C. Maurice Cherry
Furman University

Carol Wilkerson
Western Kentucky University

Selected Proceedings of the 2008 Joint Conference of the
Southern Conference on Language Teaching
and the South Carolina Foreign Language Teachers' Association

Dimension 2008: Lauguages for the Nation

© 2008 Southern Conference on Language Teaching

Lynne McClendon, Executive Director
165 Lazy Laurel Chase
Roswell, GA 30076
Telephone 770-992-1256
Fax 770-992-3464
http://www.scolt.org
lynnemcc@mindspring.com

All rights reserved. No part of this book may be reproduced,
in any form or by any means, without
written permission from the publisher.

ISBN 1-883640-22-9

Carolyn L. Hansen
DLLC-Spanish Program
University of South Carolina
Columbia, SC 29208

TABLE OF CONTENTS

Review and Acceptance Procedures iv
2008 SCOLT Editorial Board v
Introduction vii
Acknowledgments x

1 Drama in the Classroom
and Improved Academic Performance 1
Dennis R. Miller, Jr.

2 An Analysis of the Teaching Proficiency
Through Reading and Storytelling (TPRS) Method.................................13
David Alley and Denise Overfield

3 Technoconstructivism and the Millennial Generation:
Creative Writing in the Foreign Language Classroom 27
Edwina Spodark

4 Technology for Oral Assessment...39
Patricia Early and Peter B. Swanson

5 The Teacher Work Sample
in Foreign Language Education 49
Marat Sanatullov

6 Connecting a Standards-Based Curriculum
with Student Performance and Assessment...63
Rosalie Cheatham

7 The National Security Language Initiative
and Less Commonly Taught Languages..81
Elvira Sanatullova-Allison

8 The Belgian Connection 97
Lisa Signori

SCOLT Board of Directors 113
Advisory Board: Individual Sponsors, 2007 114
Advisory Board: Patrons Representing Institutions and Organizations .. 116
Previous Issues of *Dimension*: Ordering Information 119

Review and Acceptance Procedures
SCOLT *Dimension*

The procedures through which articles are reviewed and accepted for publication in the proceedings volume of the Southern Conference on Language Teaching (SCOLT) begin with the submission of a proposal to present a session at the SCOLT Annual Conference. Once the members of the Program Committee have made their selections, the editors invite each presenter to submit the abstract of an article that might be suitable for publication in *Dimension*, the annual volume of conference proceedings.

Only those persons who present *in person* at the annual Joint Conference are eligible to have written versions of their presentations included in *Dimension*. Those whose abstracts are accepted receive copies of publication guidelines, which adhere almost entirely to the fifth edition of the *Publication Manual of the American Psychological Association*. The names and academic affiliations of the authors and information identifying schools and colleges cited in articles are removed from the manuscripts, and at least three members of the Editorial Board and the two editors review each of them. Reviewers, all of whom are professionals committed to second language education, make one of four recommendations: "publish as is," "publish with minor revisions," "publish with significant rewriting," or "do not publish."

The editors review the recommendations and notify all authors as to whether their articles will be printed. As a result of these review procedures, at least three individuals decide whether to include an oral presentation in the annual conference, and at least five others read and evaluate each article that appears in *Dimension*.

2008 SCOLT Editorial Board

Theresa A. Antes
University of Florida
Gainesville, FL

Jean-Pierre Berwald
University of Massachusetts,
  emeritus
Amherst, MA

Lee Bradley
Valdosta State University, emeritus
Valdosta, GA

Paula Heusinkveld
Clemson University
Clemson, SC

Norbert Hedderich
University of Rhode Island
Kingston, RI

Shawn Morrison
College of Charleston
Charleston, SC

Jean Marie Schultz
University of California
  at Santa Barbara
Santa Barbara, CA

Louise Stanford
South Carolina Governor's School
  for the Arts and Humanities,
  retired
Greenville, SC

Toni Theisen
Loveland High School
Fort Collins, CO

Helene Zimmer-Loew
American Association of
  Teachers of German
Cherry Hill, NJ

Introduction

The Southern Conference on Language Teaching (SCOLT), held its annual conference, April 3-5, 2008, at the Springmaid Beach Resort and Conference Center, in Myrtle Beach, South Carolina, in collaboration with the South Carolina Foreign Language Teachers' Association (SCFLTA). The SCOLT Board of Directors chose as this year's theme, "Languages for the Nation," because it suggested opportunities for language professionals to develop presentations on a wide array of topics. Those whose presentations were approved were given the opportunity to submit an abstract for an article for possible inclusion in *Dimension 2008*. The articles selected for the present volume treat topics of interest to language teachers in a variety of ways. Some provide updates on timely issues of interest to the profession; others shed light on significant topics that are occasionally overlooked; and a few provide novel treatments of familiar subjects.

In "Drama in the Classroom and Improved Academic Performance," Dennis R. Miller discusses an unusual experience provided to three distinct groups of students in intermediate-level college Spanish courses. Students in a university setting with a fairly traditional student body, others at a historically African-American university, and a third group made up of inmates in a correctional institution all read, analyzed, and performed the same Nicaraguan one-act play. Miller shares with readers details of the classroom performance and the reactions of students in all three groups both before and after the performance. That the experience had a positive impact on the linguistic development of the participants is perhaps not surprising; however, Miller learned that the benefits of the performance were equally important through their impact on students' self-esteem and their motivation for continuing their study of Spanish.

"Total Physical Response," or TPR, continues to be part of the repertoire of language teachers some 40 years after its introduction. Recently, educators have incorporated elements of storytelling into this approach, changing the name to "Teaching Proficiency Through Reading and Storytelling," or TPRS. Although the name change is relatively new, David Alley and Denise Overfield find that the principles underlying TPRS have more in common with older, more traditional, grammar-based teaching strategies than with today's learner-focused, communicative strategies. Their article, "An Analysis of the Teaching Proficiency Through Reading and Storytelling (TPRS) Method," describes the basic tenets of TPRS and concludes that considerations of culture, comparisons, connections, communities, and, to some degree, content are secondary to the development of listening comprehension and oral proficiency.

Each generation of students seems to have unique characteristics and learning styles. Today's so-called "Millennials," those born about the time the personal computer was introduced, prefer learning environments that simultaneously allow for individual creativity and peer collaboration; and they prefer to be taught by faculty who are highly adept in using information technology. Edwina Spodark finds that *technoconstructivism* best suits the personality and learning needs of Millennials. This approach to teaching combines the tenets of social constructivism with proficiency in technology. In her article, "Technoconstructivism and the Millennial Generation: Creative Writing in the Foreign Language Classroom," Spodark shares a protocol she uses in a fifth-semester, university French course. Students collaborate to create stories and legends of francophone countries; they serve as peer reviewers and editors while the stories are written; and they become the audience during presentations of the stories. The strategies that Spodark describes may inspire other language instructors who seek to enhance the use of technology in their classrooms.

The changing role of technology in language teaching is also the focus of "Technology for Oral Assessment." The authors, Patricia Early and Peter Swanson, offer a review of different hardware, software, and Webware resources particularly suited to oral assessment. They also describe a study comparing traditional, in-class oral assessment with oral assessment using technology. Findings indicate that rehearsal time increased and speech was more authentic when students recorded their answers outside of class. Additionally, faculty reported that technology enhanced rater reliability and allowed for greater flexibility in grading than did traditional, in-class oral assessment.

The Teacher Work Sample (TWS) has become a fairly standard component of teacher education programs throughout the nation and is frequently cited as an important tool for assessing the strength of individual candidates. In "The Teacher Work Sample in Foreign Language Education," Marat Sanatullov provides detailed information on how to use the TWS to document both the pre-service teachers' requisite knowledge base to plan instruction and their success in teaching the content. In addition, Sanatullov explains the use of the Practice Teacher Work Sample, a preliminary version of the TWS devised to serve as a preliminary assessment of the pre-service candidate's understanding of foreign language standards, proficiency-based instruction, and best practices.

Rosalie Cheatham outlines the ways in which her university's language department rethought its French curriculum to address as honestly as possible the need for those in post-secondary institutions to make the "standards" an integral part of their entire major program. "Connecting a Standards-Based Curriculum with Student Performance and Assessment" offers a rationale for effecting such changes and provides substantial details concerning the implementation of the reform. Of particular interest to readers will be the precise ways in which the Five Cs (Communication, Cultures, Comparisons, Communities, and Connections) serve as the organizing principle for the structure of the revised curriculum. Underlying the design as well is the department's attention to the key elements of the Integrated Performance Assessment—the interpretive, interpersonal, and presentational modes.

September 11, 2001, remains a pivotal point in recent American history. Five years later, in 2006, President George W. Bush introduced the National Security Language Initiative (NSLI), which identified a number of less commonly taught languages as being critical to national security and prosperity. In "The National Security Language Initiative and Less Commonly Taught Languages," Elvira Sanatullova-Allison defines critical and less commonly taught languages, and she describes the unique challenges faced by those who study, teach, and aspire to teach these languages. Sanatullova-Allison calls for public awareness to work toward equity and advocacy for less commonly taught languages.

French teachers at all levels have on occasion been criticized for emphasizing so greatly the language and culture of France that they apparently overlook opportunities to connect their students to other key francophone areas throughout the world. In recent years both publishers and classroom teachers have made significant strides in introducing students to francophone culture the world over— in Africa, the Caribbean, Quebec, and various Pacific islands. In "The Belgian Connection," Lisa Signori, while applauding these efforts to expose students of French to diverse areas where the language is spoken, argues that the area of Belgium known as Wallonia is, unfortunately, still overlooked by most teachers of French. Her panoply of cultural snapshots of Belgium includes discussions of the history, cuisine, arts, and popular culture of the country, with special attention to the linguistic and cultural phenomena that distinguish Wallonia from the rest of the nation. She concludes her article with suggestions for ways that teachers of French can integrate this information in meaningful ways into their lessons plans.

As editors of *Dimension 2008,* we hope that readers of the articles in this volume will find the work of these authors as captivating and informative as we did. We call your particular attention to a preceding section, "Review and Acceptance Procedures," and remind readers that the deadline of April 15, 2008, is set for the submission of proposals for the 2009 SCOLT Conference in Atlanta, Georgia. We urge readers to consider preparing a proposal for a presentation at our 2009 conference and remind them that those whose articles are accepted will be eligible to develop their presentations into articles for possible inclusion in next year's volume of conference proceedings.

The Editors

C. Maurice CherryCarol Wilkerson
Furman UniversityWestern Kentucky University
Greenville, SCBowling Green, KY

Acknowledgments

Like any collection of articles, *Dimension 2008* is a collaborative effort. Foremost among the key players are the authors, who hail from nine colleges and universities in six states and without whom there would be no publication. Each of their submissions was carefully read by the co-editors and several members of the Editorial Board, all of whom assisted in the process of selecting the articles to be included and recommended varying degrees and types of revisions. Some manuscripts needed amplification or condensation; a few called for clarification of words or documentation; and still others required updating of data or Web sites. To a person, the authors responded in a timely and positive fashion, and the editors would be hard-pressed to find a more cooperative group of writers.

Equally deserving of accolades are the Editorial Board members, foreign language professionals representing diverse fields and institutions in eight states, five of which are located beyond the SCOLT region. All reviewers carefully evaluated several articles, suggested additional resources that needed to be consulted, requested clarification of ambiguous words or ideas, cited needed corrections, and recommended other changes they felt would enhance the quality of the publication. Although the authors understood that they were under no obligation to accept all of the recommendations, they typically incorporated most of them into their articles and expressed their gratitude for the advice being rendered.

In this, my tenth and final year of service as editor or co-editor of *Dimension*, I convey my gratitude to Lynne McClendon, SCOLT's Executive Director, for her continued support of my efforts. I also offer my wholehearted thanks to my mentor, Lee Bradley, an emeritus faculty member of Valdosta State University, my co-editor for several issues of *Dimension*, and publisher of all previous issues during my tenure and for many volumes prior to my having been named editor.

It is now my privilege to pass the mantle to Carol Wilkerson, my co-editor for *Dimension 2008* and the editor for subsequent volumes. Over the past few months she has already demonstrated both a discerning eye for detail and an acute awareness of what is needed in a professional publication. Carol has further proved to be a tireless worker, one endowed with warmth and a wonderful sense of humor, traits that will serve her well as she assumes her new position.

With this issue, *Dimension* welcomes aboard Carolyn Hansen, who has accepted the post of publisher, a role held so ably by Lee Bradley for many years. A long-time faculty member at USC-Columbia, Carolyn brings to this venture considerable leadership experience in many areas, particularly as a former member of the SCOLT Board and as Executive Director of the South Carolina Foreign Language Teachers' Association (SCFLTA), our co-host for this year's conference.

Finally, I would be remiss if I failed to acknowledge the support of my wife Sharon during my decade-long journey. A leader in our profession in her own right, she has been unduly patient with me over the years as I have requested time to take yet one more look at a manuscript or to reformat an article. For her understanding, I am indeed grateful.

C. Maurice Cherry, Co-Editor
Furman University

1

Drama in the Classroom and Improved Academic Performance

Dennis R. Miller, Jr.
Morehouse College

Abstract

Educators are generally aware of the importance of using authentic texts reflecting real-world situations in the language classroom. Tarone & Swain (1995) argue that contextualized materials that reflect nonacademic settings are highly beneficial in the language classroom and increase student proficiency. This article examines the effects of using an unedited Nicaraguan play on student self-esteem and motivation by comparing second-semester Spanish classes that performed the play to those that did not. Three very different student environments are examined: a large, primarily White state university; a men's correctional facility; and a private, historically African-American college. All students involved in the study completed surveys, and, as originally suspected, student motivation increased for the classes that staged the play. In addition, these students reaped long-term benefits, as reflected in their overall higher academic achievement.

Background

In the last few decades the shift from a teacher- to a student-centered classroom has increased the overall communicative competence of students studying a second language (L2). Educators now, more than ever, strive to create lively classes based on a communicative curriculum. Savignon (2002) believes that "a truly communicative curriculum is made up of five categories: language analysis, language for a purpose, personal second language use, second language use outside the classroom, and theater arts" (p. 11).

Theater is particularly useful in a language classroom for a variety of reasons. As many studies suggest, the greater the authenticity of the texts used in the classroom, the higher the learner's competency (Omaggio, 2001; Lacorte & Canabal, 2002). In fact, using unedited, truly authentic texts tends to increase competency and reduce anxieties in real-world communicative contexts (Auger & Valdman, 1999; Genesee, 1987). By reading plays and subsequently acting them out, students are indirectly exposed to different registers, exemplifying differences between both classroom and non-classroom discourse and dialects. More importantly, students realize that languages are part of heterogeneous, plural communities, vital in the globalized 21st century. Authentic texts, such as plays, should become increasingly important components of L2 classrooms, where language is viewed as a whole, not as bits of noncommunicative chunks (Goodman, 1986).

A play can certainly alter students' preconceived notions of language learning: conjugating verbs, memorizing grammar rules, completing uncontextualized worksheets, the traditional form-focused tasks. Once the classroom is transformed into a "dramatic world," students are able to focus on the play's meaning, as opposed to its form, an advantage that encompasses two of Berns's (1990) principles of Communicative Language Teaching (CLT). She reminds us that "language teaching is based on a view of language as communication" (p. 104). During the dramatic process, students must completely concentrate on their lines and those their classmates read. As a result, grammar becomes a secondary concern at best, if at all. More importantly, according to Berns, is the requirement of CLT that "learners should be engaged in doing things with the language" (p. 104). Even in its rawest form, theater is nothing but a "doing" activity. Students are setting up the scenery, performing roles, or listening to the play's "characters" perform. Through entertainment, theater assures that each student is an active learner. Whether or not each student has a role, the entire class is engaged in the communicative process.

Most L2 teachers already use a common feature of theater in their classrooms—role-playing. It has long been established that role-play can reduce student anxiety, even among the most timid students. As students enter the realm of fantasy, they become someone besides themselves, through a form of "dissociation," or what Hancock (1997) refers to as "breaking frame." Because of this temporary escape, the anxiety levels of the students decrease, producing a highly conducive learning environment, an important component of Krashen's (1982) "Monitor Model." A classroom in which several plays are performed throughout the school year (or semester) can produce lower anxiety levels, possibly higher grades, and an increased level of student participation. Wang (2002) believes this type of environment creates "fear-reduced learning" and that "positive experiences at the beginning stage often build up confidence and result in ultimate success" (p. 139). This confidence-building strategy can inevitably lead to life-long language learning, the goal of every L2 teacher.

The *Standards for Foreign Language in the 21st Century* (National Standards in Foreign Language Education Project, 1999) delineates three specific communicative modes: interpretive, presentational, and interpersonal. Theater, along with other forms of communication, is an excellent example of all three. In the interpretive mode, students are forced to negotiate meaning when they read the text by themselves, perform it, or see it staged, since they are unable to ask the writers for clarification. In addition, since most authentic texts are rich in cultural references, students must decode the cultural signs as well, thereby exposing themselves to the target cultures. Because of its very nature, theater also exemplifies the presentational mode. Students can present a play to their classmates. Third, whether students are reading a play or watching it being performed, they utilize the interpersonal mode, because there is both written and spoken dialogue.

The Project: Description and Method

The author has been extensively involved with theater throughout most of his life and can personally attest to theater's utility in the L2 classroom. To study this perceived outcome on college-level students, the effects of performing a play on student perception and achievement in second-semester Spanish language classrooms (Group A) were compared to those on students at the same level who did not perform a play (Group B). For the purpose of this study, a single play was used to determine whether performing just one would have a measurable influence on student motivation and performance.

First, three different classroom settings were compared: (1) Lamar University, a large state school; (2) a men's correctional facility, where men were completing college requirements while being incarcerated; and (3) Morehouse College, a historically African-American male college. Three very diverse settings were selected in order to determine whether or not the results would be vastly different, as the demographics of the classes were heterogeneous and representative of the population at large. However, the manner in which students were assessed was identical, as the final grade was broken down into the following categories: Participation, 15%; Quizzes/Exams, 35%; Midterm, 15%; Two Oral Exams, 10%; Two Compositions, 10%; and the Final Exam, 15%. The study was conducted over a period of nearly 3 years (Fall 2004–Spring 2007). The play, *En el hospital*, was examined and performed around midterm to assure that the learners were comfortable with one another and with the classroom setting in general. During the subsequent class period, Group A completed a survey regarding their experiences (Appendix A). Group B completed another survey (Appendix B), also at the middle of the semester, about their classroom experiences in general. The survey for Group A (Appendix A) varies only slightly from that for Group B. Items 1, 2, and 5 under section II pertain to the experiences the students had with the play to determine how performing it affected overall student motivation. Questions 1, 2, and 5 for the group that did not perform the play (Group B) were more general in nature. All other questions on the survey were identical for both groups.

This study sought to answer four basic inquiries regarding the use of theater in the second-semester language classroom and its effects on language acquisition: (1) Does using theater in the classroom have any effects on self-esteem, either positive or negative? (2) How can unedited, authentic texts produce a greater interest in studying Hispanic cultures and the Spanish language in general? (3) Does a comparison of the results from Group A and Group B in this study lead to any type of conclusion regarding the use of drama as part of a communicative curriculum? Finally, (4) How do learners perceive the use of theater in second-semester Spanish classes?

The biggest challenge was selecting the most appropriate play for the students, as many collections of plays tailored for Spanish language classrooms are highly effective (for an excellent collection of plays, see Lozano, 2003). There are also many effective plays found in the Latin American journal *Conjunto*. The author's previous work with Nicaraguan theater led him to select a short Nicaraguan skit, *En el hospital,* collectively written by the theater group Teatro Mazatepelt (1980). There are several pedagogical justifications for using this play. First, it utilizes the Five Cs described in the *Standards for Foreign Language Education in the 21st century* (National Standards, 1999). The Five Cs in this case can be used to describe what the learners can do with the language presented after reading the play and focusing on form and especially on meaning. By using a variety of prereading activities and comprehension checks, the instructor may ensure that the play fundamentally engages students in the use of Spanish (*Communication*), as the emphasis quickly shifts from form to content. The play censures the futility of the Nicaraguan health care system (*Cultures/Connections*), a concern that is becoming increasingly prevalent in the United States (*Comparisons*). The study of this text easily lends itself to further student research as to why healthcare is a concern in both the U.S. and Latin America. When feasible conditions permitted, students were asked to complete research with Hispanics in their local communities about this important social issue (*Communities*). From the prelistening activities, to the discussion of the play, and in the postperformance activities, Spanish can be used exclusively. English is necessary only should clarification questions arise regarding the play's use of colloquial Nicaraguan Spanish.

Besides its socially relevant theme, *En el hospital* was selected because it dramatizes the reality of Nicaragua, a country often marginalized in many Spanish language texts. The use of Nicaraguan Spanish presents the students with a register to which they are probably not accustomed. Research suggests that students are more successful when exposed to the greatest number of dialects, including "non-bookish" varieties (Auger, 2002; Daniel, 2000; Draper & Hicks, 2000; Hidalgo, 1997; Shrum & Glisan, 2000). The play is deliberately written in vernacular, non-academic Spanish, a rejection of traditional, hypercorrect academic Spanish. *En el hospital* is a three-page skit; and although some students thought work on the play would be an easy task because of its brevity, the theme and rich cultural references provide a large number of linguistic and cultural codes.

Also, even though the play presents a very serious theme, it does so humorously, keeping the action interesting and relevant. Several grammatical points typically studied—such as stem-changing verbs, reflexive verbs, and the preterit—are contained in the text. After the students read the play and see it performed, there is little need to focus on the form of the language because of the play's context (Krashen, 1982). Many scholars have previously studied the effectiveness of implicit grammatical instruction, which can be taken advantage of with this play (consult, for example, Dulay & Burt, 1973; Herron & Tomasello, 1992; Terrell, 1997; Vavra, 1996). The language educator could easily pose questions requiring manipulation of specific forms without having students realize that they are practicing grammar.

Finally, *En el hospital* dispels learners' notions of what constitutes theater—usually, extravagant Broadway productions. Since this play was composed specifically for the lower classes, those most affected by lack of health care, no props are required; therefore, little energy is expended on production. Because *En el hospital* also requires an active audience, the students who do not participate in the play's staging must be engaged in the process by closely listening and then discussing the play's possible content and significance afterwards. The combined production and post-performance discussion generally requires between 20 and 50 minutes.

A similar approach was used for each of the teaching environments. The students were told in the preceding class period that they would be reading a short dramatic skit that would be performed during the following class meeting. The class then made a list of their perceptions about Nicaragua and the country's health care system. They were told to read the text for the following class and to think about the global meaning presented. At the next session, after the class presented a brief summary, various students were selected to perform the roles. The play was presented twice, and, as indicated in the stage directions, the students were to engage the audience in dialogue regarding the play's relevance. The various reactions expressed, as well as possible conclusions, were written on the blackboard. Students were then asked to write a short paragraph in Spanish comparing the health care system presented in this text to what they have encountered in the United States. In all three venues, the conclusions were strikingly similar. Also, all the information presented in class, from the prelistening activities to the postperformance dialogue, appeared in the cultural section on the subsequent exam. Students overwhelmingly did well on that section, thereby indicating that they were engaged throughout the process.

The study began at Lamar University because the second-semester Spanish classes there were representative of the types of university classrooms found in most of the United States. The majority of the classes were composed primarily of female students (typically 65% female vs. 35% male) and represented a wide array of students: non-traditional students (working mothers, students employed full-time) and a variety of traditional students. Although this environment was the most heterogeneous, the results of the survey were similar. The play was well-received, possibly because the nursing major is very common at this university.

After performing this study at Lamar University for two semesters, the author selected as participants two second-semester Spanish classes at a local men's correctional facility, where instruction was provided through a two-year college. His intent was to examine another group of students as part of the study. Even though Miller (2005) suggests that a truly communicative approach can be challenging in non-traditional settings, the same format was used with nearly the same level of success. Although all the students were male (100%), the population was still diverse in many ways. Students were from a variety of economic and educational backgrounds, but the overall motivational level was higher than that found at Lamar University, because for these learners, being able to take a college-level course was a privilege afforded to few. In this prison setting the students often maintained more decorum than in the other two institutions. Also, guards dissuade instructors from yielding too much power to the learners. At any rate, the classes were receptive to the play because of the limited access to health care in the correctional facility setting. Those from economically disadvantaged backgrounds were able to empathize with the characters unable to get access to health care. As a result, many of the students were highly critical of the health care system presented. Chávez (2002) argues that the "learner's beliefs are central in communicative, learner-centered approaches" (p. 164), a phenomenon most evident in the two classes involved at this particular correctional facility. Because the majority already believed that the health care system was flawed, the play was not as shocking as it was to the students beyond the prison setting. Because the learners did not have Internet access, they were unable to gather any information on health care systems, a circumstance that did not inhibit the learners from engaging in a highly communicative activity. In fact, many did not hesitate to express in the target language their frustration regarding health care in the U.S. The fact that most of the pre- and postperformance discussions were conducted in Spanish exemplifies the importance of incorporating socially-relevant themes in the L2 classroom.

Finally, the most recent study was that completed in 2006 and 2007 at Morehouse College, a historically all-male African-American college. It should be noted that all three settings had nearly the same variety of majors, as well as reasons why students opted to study Spanish. In contrast to Lamar University, the classes at Morehouse College are overwhelmingly male (97% male vs. 3 % female), yet the student body was as varied as in the other settings. Theater and "doing theater" have been viewed historically and academically as a feminine, emasculating activity (see Miller, 2003, in particular, pp. 1- 2). Fortunately, this was not the case for the majority of the male students in any of the venues. The same format was followed as in the other second-semester Spanish classes. The postperformance discussions led to lively discussions primarily in Spanish that shifted from a critique of the Nicaraguan health care system to the current health care crisis in the United States and possible solutions.

The Results

A total of 343 students from Lamar University, the male correctional facility, and Morehouse College (Group A) completed the survey (Appendix A) that attempted to determine how learners perceived the process. In all settings and classes, the students at the three academic settings had overwhelmingly favorable experiences with the play and the way in which it was used in class: 85% highly agreed that the play was a worthwhile activity, while only about 3% felt it was not a valuable use of time. The specific reactions regarding the use of the play for the three different settings are detailed in the following graph (Group A):

	Very effective	Moderately effective	Somewhat effective	Not at all effective
Lamar University	80%	10%	5%	5%
Male Correctional Facility	85%	11%	1%	3%
Morehouse College	91%	7%	0%	2%

The instructor impressed upon the students participating in the play that this activity would be highly beneficial to their overall acquisition process. However, many L2 scholars have stressed that what motivates a student is often personal, and that learner and teacher perceptions of the importance of particular activities are often diametrically opposed (for example, Gardner, 1985; Oxford & Shearin, 1994; Wen, 1997). The students who did not participate in the play comprise Group B. Group A and Group B had different reactions to the class as a whole. Surveys (Appendix B) were also given to Group B, and the learners in these classes had slightly less favorable perceptions of the class. The learners in both groups were exposed to an equally enthusiastic, student-centered classroom, and it is interesting to note that the two groups had somewhat different perceptions of classroom realities. Group B consisted of 321 students. Of these, 65% (20% lower than for Group A) had an extremely favorable reaction to the communicative classroom created, while, as demonstrated in Appendix B, 5% (2% higher than for Group A) had a very negative impression of the Spanish language and classroom. The following table demonstrates the less positive reactions of the students who did not perform the play (Group B) toward their second-semester Spanish class:

	Very effective	Moderately effective	Somewhat effective	Not at all effective
Lamar University	58%	25%	7%	10%
Male Correctional Facility	66%	27%	3%	4%
Morehouse College	70%	25%	4%	1%

There were no perceptible differences between the three different testing sites (Lamar University, the male correctional facility, and Morehouse College) that comprised Group A.

Another very unexpected result of this study was overall class performance. Midterm grades (prior to the play's performance) for Group A (the three different sites combined) were as follows: A: 25%, B: 20%, C: 30%, D: 15%, and F: 10%. The midterm grades for Group B, which did not perform the play, were: A: 25%, B: 28%, C: 33%, D: 8%, and F: 6%. Group A performed better academically the rest of the semester. The overall breakdown of final grades for students in Group A is as follows: A: 35%, B: 30%, C: 25%, D: 5%, and F: 5%. Students in Group B did not fare quite as well: A: 20%, B: 25%, C: 27%, D: 17%, and F: 11%. In fact, the grades for Group B actually declined after the midterm. Group A excelled better orally. For example, the students had a slightly higher level of oral competency in the oral exams they presented after the play. Group A also did better on the oral components on written exams and, overall, seemed more eager to use the target language in class as much as possible.

The surveys themselves could possibly be reflections of a very positive classroom activity, especially since students completed the surveys for the classes that performed the play during the class period following the performance. Some of the student comments on the surveys—such as "I feel more comfortable with Spanish after performing the play," "I feel less shy in class now," and "Let's do more plays"—also attest to the positive effect performing a play can have on student motivation and academic performance. The higher grades suggest that motivation levels remained higher the rest of the semester, an additional 7 weeks. It should also be noted that students included positive comments regarding the play on the blind student evaluations completed at the end of the semester. When asked what they enjoyed most about the course, students provided such comments as "I liked doing the play," "I hope I can do theater in my next Spanish class," "I never did plays in Spanish until this class," and "Thanks for the play," providing examples of the positive experience they had with this project.

Possible Explanations of Results

While an infinite number of factors can determine a student's perception of any given class, several possibilities exist that may offer insight into the disparity between the results for Group A and Group B. Cooperative learning is often an integral part of most communicative language classrooms, and such was the case here on a grander scale. The entire project required cooperative learning, whether in the performance of the play, negotiation of meaning as a collective group, or the determination by the class of the text's significance. It has been shown that large-scale projects, such as class performance of a play, can increase overall motivation, self-esteem, and interest in the language studied (Johnson & Johnson, 1989). Is it possible that one-and-a-half positive class periods produced long-lasting, increased levels of motivation and higher grades overall? If so, how?

The answer may lie in the use of theater itself. Plays have often been used as a form of pedagogy, particularly outside the U.S. As students become engaged in decoding the text's meaning, an aspect of U.S. culture can become denaturalized, forcing them to examine our own system. Theater scholar Dolan (2001) believes that theater can "move us toward understanding the possibility of something better, can train our imaginations, inspire our dreams and fuel our possibilities in ways that might lead to incremental cultural change" (p. 460). Such is one of the basic premises of the renowned master of pedagogy, Freire (1993): the notion of *conscientização* (consciousness-raising), training students to be active thinkers, not passive recipients of knowledge. Perhaps it was this consciousness-raising the play required of the students that caused them to become more motivated and to excel academically. Students became critical thinkers and most likely continued to view the world critically the rest of the semester. During the performance and various postperformance activities, students who generally did not speak in class spoke and in many instances became extremely active participants in discussions, most of which occurred in the target language. Through dialogue like the ones that ensued, students learned that problems can possibly be resolved. The students in Group A consistently stated that they were interested in performing more plays the remainder of the semester. This reaction is perhaps a testament to the power of theater and, by extension, to the use of authentic, interesting texts in general.

Conclusions

The study sought to determine whether having students involved in the performance of an authentic Nicaraguan play would have any effect on student motivation, self-esteem, and overall academic achievement. The results demonstrated that there was a correlation between higher academic achievement in second-semester Spanish classes (Group A) and the use of drama in the classroom. The most noticeable effect was a higher level of student motivation in the classes at all three university settings, particularly among the quieter, more introverted students.

This article indirectly poses more questions and necessitates more studies by the author and other language teachers. What are the long-term effects on students' future language study? The positive student comments on the surveys (Appendix A) and student evaluations completed at the end of the semester coupled with higher academic performance certainly argue for the use of perhaps several plays throughout the semester. Had more plays been studied, would the students' motivation, oral competency and grammatical accuracy subsequently have continued to rise? While there is a point in which too many plays would make the class too predicable and lacking in variety, performing several throughout the semester would, most likely, have an overall beneficial effect on the students. The results of this study should be encouraging to all language educators. More plays from a variety of Spanish and Latin American settings could easily be incorporated into any Spanish-language classroom. In fact, it can be concluded that when more authentic texts, like socially-relevant plays, radio broadcasts, and soap operas, are incorporated into a classroom setting, a more productive, communicative environment will be created.

Finally, perhaps after using a play such as *En el hospital*, students may collaborate as a class or in groups and write their own script to be presented to the class, Spanish Club, or the community at large, especially for a Hispanic audience. After their experience with this play, students could collaborate on drama projects within their local Hispanic communities and present them at a later time, establishing a vital connection between language, culture, and community.

References

Auger, J. (2002). Linguistic norm vs. functional competence: Introducing Québec French to American students. In C. Blyth (Ed.), *The sociolinguistics of foreign language classrooms* (pp. 79-104). Boston: Thomson & Heinle.

Auger, J., & Valdman, A. (1999). Letting French students hear the diverse voices of Francophony. *Modern Language Journal, 83*, 403-412.

Berns, M. (1990). *Contexts of competence: Sociocultural considerations in communicative language teaching.* New York: Plenum.

Chávez, M. (2002). The diglossic foreign-language classroom: Learners' views on L1 and L2 functions. In C. Blyth (Ed.), *The sociolinguistics of foreign-language classrooms* (pp. 163-201). Boston: Thomson & Heinle.

Daniel, J. (2000). Speak my language: Open the window to my heart, to my conscience, to my intelligence. In J. Webb and B. Miller (Eds.), *Teaching heritage language learners: Voices from the classroom* (pp. 176-82). Yonkers, NY: ACTFL.

Dolan, J. (2001). Performance, utopia, and the "utopian performative." *Theatre Journal, 53*, 455-79.

Draper, J., & Hicks, J. (2000). Where we've been; what we've learned. In J. Webb and B.Miller (Eds.), *Teaching heritage language learners: Voices from the classroom* (pp. 15-35). Yonkers, NY: ACTFL.

Dulay, J., & Burt, M. (1973). Should we teach children syntax? *Language Learning, 23*, 245-258.

Freire, P. (1993). *Pedagogy of the oppressed.* Trans. Myra Bergman Ramos. New York: Continuum.

Gardner, R. C. (1985). *Social psychology and second language learning: The role of attitudes and motivation.* London, Ontario: Edward Arnold.

Genesee, F. (1987). *Learning through two languages: Studies of immersion and bilingual education.* Cambridge, MA: Newbury House.

Goodman, K. (1986). *What's whole in whole language.* Portsmouth, NH: Heineman Educational Books.

Hancock, M. (1997). Behind classroom code switching: Layering and language choice in L2 learner interaction. *TESOL Quarterly, 31*, 217-235.

Herron, C., & Tomasello, M. (1992). Acquiring grammatical structures by guided induction. *The French Review, 65,* 708-718.

Hidalgo, M. (1997). Criterios normativos e ideología lingüística: Aceptación y rechazo del español de los Estados Unidos. In F. Alarcón and M. Colombi (Eds.) *La enseñanza del español a hispanohablantes: Praxis y teoría* (pp.109- 120). Boston: Houghton Mifflin.

Johnson, D. W., & Johnson, R. T. (1989). *Cooperation and competition: Theory and research.* Edina, MN: Interaction Book Company.

Krashen, S. (1982). *Principles and practice in second language acquisition.* Oxford, England: Pergamon Press.

Lacorte, L., & Canabal, E. (2002). Interaction with heritage language learners in foreign language classrooms. In C. Blyth (Ed.), *The sociolinguistics of foreign-language classrooms* (pp. 107-129). Boston: Thomson & Heinle.

Lozano, P. (2003). *Teatro de cuento de hadas.* Houston, TX: Dolo Publications.

Miller, D. (2003). Nicaraguan theater of the twentieth century: A closer evaluation. *Dissertation Abstracts International, 64,* 07A.

Miller, D. (2005). Prison instruction and second language acquisition: The practicality of recent theorizing in non-traditional settings. *Texas Foreign Language Association Bulletin, 16*(1), 25-28.

National Standards in Foreign Language Education Project. (1999). *Standards for foreign language learning in the 21st century.* Yonkers, NY: Author.

Omaggio, A. (2001). *Teaching language in context.* 2nd ed. Boston: Heinle & Heinle.

Oxford, R., & Shearin, J. (1994). Language learning motivation: Expanding the theoretical framework. *The Modern Language Journal, 73,* 291-300.

Savignon, S. (2002). Communicative language teaching: Linguistic theory and classroom practice. In S. Savignon (Ed.), *Interpreting communicative language teaching* (pp. 1-27). New Haven, CT: Yale University Press.

Shrum, J. L., & Glisan, E. W. (2000). *Teacher's handbook: Contextualized language instruction.* Boston: Heinle & Heinle.

Teatro Mazatepelt. (1980). En el hospital. *Conjunto, 45,* 44-46.

Tarone, E., & Swain, M. (1995). A sociolinguistic perspective on second language use in immersion classrooms. *Modern Language Journal, 79,* 166-178.

Terrell, T. (1977). A natural approach to second-language acquisition and learning. *The Modern Language Journal, 61,* 325-337.

Vavra. E. (1996). On not teaching grammar. *English Journal, 85*(7), 32-37.

Wang, C. (2002). Innovative teaching in Taiwan. In S. Savignon (Ed.), *Interpreting communicative language teaching* (pp. 131-153). New Haven, CT: Yale University Press.

Wen, X. (1997). Motivation and language learning with students of Chinese. *Foreign Language Annals, 30,* 235-251.

Appendix A

General Survey (completed between fall 2004 and spring 2007)

I. General information:

(a) What is your major?
(b) Please list the Spanish courses you have taken previously:
(c) What grades do you generally receive in your Spanish courses?

II. Rate the following statements from 1 to 5, with "5" being "I strongly agree," and "1" the equivalent of "I strongly disagree."

1. Theater got me interested in the Spanish language. _____
2. After this play I wanted to learn more about Nicaragua. _____
3. I am now more interested in studying in a Spanish-speaking country. _____
4. I feel more comfortable speaking Spanish. _____
5. I would like to do more plays in my Spanish language classes. _____

III. Please respond to the following questions:

1. What have you enjoyed the most about this class thus far? The least?
2. Why are you studying Spanish?

Appendix B

General Survey (completed between fall 2004 and spring 2007)

I. General information:

    (a) What is your major?
    (b) Please list the Spanish courses you have taken previously:
    (c) What grades do you generally receive in your Spanish courses?

II. Rate the following statements from 1 to 5, with "5" being "I strongly agree," and "1" the equivalent of "I strongly disagree."

    1. I enjoy learning about Hispanic cultures. _____
    2. Spanish will be helpful with my future profession. _____
    3. I am interested in studying in a Spanish-speaking country. _____
    4. I am comfortable speaking Spanish. _____
    5. As a result of this class, I'd like to continue practicing Spanish. _____

III. Please respond to the following questions:

    1. What have you enjoyed the most about this class thus far? The least?
    2. Why are you studying Spanish?

2
An Analysis of the Teaching Proficiency Through Reading and Storytelling (TPRS) Method

David Alley
Georgia Southern University

Denise Overfield
University of West Georgia

Abstract

Teaching Proficiency Through Reading and Storytelling (TPRS) is a popular method for teaching world languages that largely abandons textbooks and grammatical exercises in favor of short, humorous stories paired with physical movements. This article provides an historical context for the TPRS method, a summary of the method's procedures, and a description of the current status of the TPRS movement. Finally, the article considers the method in light of recent second language acquisition research in an effort to establish theoretical support for the enthusiastic claims of its proponents. The study reveals that TPRS has more in common with older language teaching methods than with current standards-based instruction.

Background

Like most teachers, foreign language educators are enthusiastic about their profession, but testimonies about methodology like the following are not commonplace:

> I taught French from the grammarian point of view UNTIL (yes, I am screaming) until my eyes were opened to this method. No one could have predicted that I would have changed my perspective concerning this method. I have seen the difference of teaching in this manner. I see kids, even lower level kids, succeed. I am excited. I have been teaching for 25 years. I have never seen anything like this. I only have five more years before I retire. I am having the BEST (yes, I am screaming) time I have ever had in all the years of my teaching. I didn't think I would make it through the next five years. Now I know I can. (Steele, 1997, p. 2)

Such effusive praise of Teaching Proficiency Through Reading and Storytelling (TPRS) is not unusual among its practitioners. However, with its frequent use of translation and its disavowal of the direct teaching of grammar, TPRS seems to radically break with current beliefs about effective language teaching. Yet teachers who have adopted the method report significant gains in language proficiency by their students, as well as renewed enthusiasm on their part for teaching.

The popular TPRS method for teaching world languages largely abandons textbooks in favor of simple, humorous stories illustrated with gestures and active movements. The students and teacher collaborate on the creation of each story, which presents grammatical and lexical items in context and serves as the basis for speaking, listening, reading, and writing activities. Compared to language teaching methods like Grammar Translation, the Direct Method, and the Audiolingual Method from the early part of the 20th century, TPRS appears to represent a radically different approach (Brown, 1994). However, closer examination reveals surprising similarities between TPRS and these older methodologies.

In this article, we will explore these similarities through an examination of the historical context of TPRS and other relevant teaching methodologies and will discuss how it fits with educational and second language acquisition research. We also suggest directions for further research into the effectiveness and use of TPRS.

Historical Overview

Until the latter half of the 20th century, Grammar Translation (GT) was the language teaching method of choice. GT focuses on the analysis of linguistic patterns in literary selections in order to enable students to appreciate classical and modern world literature while simultaneously improving their native language skills (Omaggio Hadley, 2001). According to Richards and Rogers (1986), however, GT rests on assumptions for which there is no theoretical basis in the fields of linguistics, psychology, or education.

The outbreak of World War II and the subsequent development of an urgent need for Americans proficient in the languages of our allies and enemies forced a re-examination of second language teaching methodology. Faced with this challenge, the United States military created intensive language courses which were based both on practices of the Direct Method (DM) as well as insights from the emerging field of psychology. The Direct Method, made famous by Charles Berlitz and his intensive language schools, was based on the premise that second language learning should closely resemble first language learning. Berlitz and other proponents of the DM devised a language teaching approach that focused on everyday situations and the use of visuals to contextualize and clarify meaning, as well as the development of listening and speaking skills through teacher-student exchanges. Grammar was taught implicitly through the formation of hypotheses and generalized grammar rules (Omaggio-Hadley, 2001). Also known as the Army Method, the DM created the framework for the Army Specialized Training Program. At the conclusion of World War II, many educational institutions began to experiment with this same method, a trend that was further accelerated by the Soviet Union's launching of the Sputnik satellite in 1957 (Brown, 1994).

Faced with the prospect of losing the space race to its Cold War rival, the United States began a massive retraining of teachers of math, science, and foreign language through the Defense Education Act of 1958. New research in behaviorist psychology, as well as continuing explorations of what might be the best way to teach language, led to the development of the Audiolingual Method (ALM). The ALM emphasizes repetitive drills to teach patterns of language, limited vocabulary taught in the context of carefully constructed dialogues, and minimal grammar explanations (Brown, 1994; Omaggio Hadley, 2001). The ALM dominated American foreign language instruction from the late 1950s until well into the 1970s. During this time, however, a new wave of research focused on children's first language acquisition and attempted to apply these new insights to second language teaching. This research gave rise to the two methodologies that are most closely related to TPRS: Total Physical Response (TPR) and the Natural Approach.

Created by psychologist James Asher, TPR gained widespread attention in the 1970s as a response to a growing public dissatisfaction with traditional language teaching. Asher (1969) theorized that listening comprehension was the basis for all other skills development (speaking, reading, and writing). Combining insights from first language acquisition and studies of the brain's right and left hemispheres, Asher contended that the basis for effective language learning is the pairing of physical responses with commands, such as "stand up, sit down, or walk to the board." Each command is first modeled by the teacher and before it is imitated by the students. Gradually the teacher ceases to model the action and the students must demonstrate their comprehension through their responses. The teacher is the primary initiator of all language use. Because of the similarity of the methodology to the way that children learn their first language, Asher hypothesized that adults studying a second language would demonstrate comparably impressive gains.

TPR gained wide popularity as an effective technique, but few language teachers accepted Asher's contention that it could be used as the basis for all second language activities. However, the premise that the explicit teaching of grammar was neither necessary nor desirable for language acquisition opened up new avenues of research that led to the development of what Nunan (2005) describes as acquisitionist approaches to language teaching, an example of which is the Natural Approach (NA), which purported to model second language learning after the universally successful way children learn their first language (Krashen & Terrell, 1983; Terrell, 1986). Unlike its predecessors that prescribed specific instructional activities, the NA focused on the development of a theory of language acquisition/learning that informed classroom practice. Shrum and Glisan (2005) summarize the five basic hypotheses that serve as the foundation for Krashen's theory:

- the acquisition-learning hypothesis, which defines acquisition as a superior, subconscious form of learning which ultimately leads to spontaneous and creative communication

- the monitor hypothesis, which characterizes the conscious, learned rules of the language as being available to the learner only under certain limited circumstances
- the natural order hypothesis, in which learners follow a predictable sequence of acquisition, rather than the order in which grammar rules have been taught
- the input hypothesis, which states that learning occurs only when learners receive comprehensible input that is slightly beyond their level of comprehension
- the affective filter hypothesis, which states that learning can occur only in an environment free of excessive anxiety and stress

Both TPR and NA are fundamentally acquisitionist approaches, or approaches that focus on meaning and not form (Nunan, 2005). Early criticism of these approaches was based on research indicating that application of grammatical and contextual rules is crucial for the development of interactional competence (see Celce-Murcia, Zoltan, & Thurrell, 1995). Swain (1985), for instance, argues that comprehensible output is at least as important as comprehensible input. According to Swain, learners must learn to shape utterances in order to create meaning. Bachman (1990) maintains that communicative language ability is not only knowledge of language, but the capacity to use that knowledge to engage in tasks. Such studies marked the beginning of an ongoing critique of the acquisitionist approaches. Concurrent with these critiques was an effort to formulate standards with which to evaluate both the product and the process of language teaching.

In the 30 years since Asher and Krashen first promoted Total Physical Response and the Natural Approach, much has happened in the field of second language teaching. The publication of the ACTFL Provisional Proficiency Guidelines (1982) replaced the overused and ambiguous term *fluency* with more accurate descriptions of levels of language proficiency. Insights gleaned from fields as seemingly diverse as anthropology, psychology, and linguistics converged to form the basis for the *Standards for Foreign Language Learning in the 21st Century* (National Standards in Foreign Language Education Project, 1999). The publication of these *Standards* established parameters for what a foreign language curriculum should include. By the late 20th century, the idea that any one method was sufficient was called into question (Salmani-Nodoushan, 2006).

All of these changes have had an impact on the development of foreign language curricula and teaching materials. However, the evolution of classroom practice depends heavily on the beliefs and creativity of educators, and for that reason changes in individual practice do not always move at the same rate or in the same direction as broader trends. The evolution of Teaching Proficiency Through Reading and Storytelling (TPRS) is one example of this phenomenon.

Total Physical Response Storytelling

In the early 1990s, Blaine Ray, a high school Spanish teacher from California who was frustrated by the mediocre progress of his students, began to experiment with Total Physical Response techniques to supplement his textbook-based and grammar-heavy lessons. To his surprise, his unmotivated students suddenly became enthusiastic, and their achievement levels rose. Eventually, however, his students grew weary of responding to endless series of commands, so; Ray continued to experiment with variations of the basic TPR idea.

> TPR worked great for the first month of the school year, but then it just ends. He (Ray) wanted to figure out how to move kids from hearing the language and responding to having the students speak in the language, generating their own sentences. He noticed that students learned the vocab [*sic*] much quicker and internalized it more through TPR than through vocab lists and exercises in the book. (Baird, Re: TPRS video, 1997)

Eventually Ray hit upon the idea of storytelling as the basis for introducing new language structures in context, and it is this approach that continues to be polished and perfected by his many followers in conferences, publications, and Internet discussions. Today the TPRS movement boasts multiple Web sites, an online professional journal, a publishing house for TPRS materials, and a national conference. A Google search of the topic *Teaching Proficiency through Reading and Storytelling* yields more than 123,000 hits, and a similar search of Google Scholar reveals more than 2,380 hits. The topic of TPRS has been the source of hundreds of comments for the last 10 years on Foreign Language Teaching Forum, a LISTSERV originating at the State University of New York College at Cortland. In a 9-month period from March to December 2007, 57 TPRS workshops were scheduled all over the United States. Clearly the TPRS movement is robust and growing.

In a first-year course, TPRS teachers use the traditional TPR method exclusively for the first several weeks. According to Asher (2007),

> There is no research that I am aware of supporting storytelling without at least three weeks of student preparation with classical TPR. After that, make a transition into storytelling but continue to use TPR for new vocabulary and grammar. This strategy applies to students of all ages and all languages. (p. 1)

During this introductory phase, students learn to comprehend approximately 150 words by repeating them and mimicking associated gestures. Throughout this initial period of TPR, the teacher constantly gauges the degree of comprehension of the new vocabulary words by monitoring *barometer students*, those middle- and low-performing students in the 20th to 40th percentile. According to Ray and Seely (1998), it is these students who should set the pace of the class. After several weeks of TPR lessons, the teacher shifts to the use of mini-situations to teach new vocabulary and practice previously learned words in novel combinations. Mini-situations are stories that contain one to four new words and phrases called *guide words,* so named because they must be used in order for a longer story to be told successfully. Each word or phrase is linked to a hand gesture and a word association. For example, to teach the Spanish word "llorar," which means 'to cry,' the teacher would pantomime the act of crying and then associate the word with the homonymic English phrase "You're a baby."

The best mini-situations are bizarre, exaggerated, and personalized (BEP in TPRS jargon). This preference for the outlandish engages the students' attention and encourages a playful, creative attitude. The teacher monitors the students' comprehension by means of personalized questions and oral fill-in-the-blank exercises. The teacher determines that the barometer students fully comprehend the new material, then narrates the story, and selects a few students to act out the mini-situation. Next, selected students take over the narration while other students act out the situation. Finally, the entire class retells the story in pairs.

Each mini-situation contributes a part to what becomes the main story. As Ray and Seely (1998) point out, "The main reason for teaching all of those mini-stories is for students to understand the main story when they hear it" (p. 58). Before teaching the main story, the teacher reviews the mini-situations and again provides either a translation or a gesture for each guide word. After this review it is time to teach the main story. Each story has at least one character, and each character has at least one problem. In an effort to solve the problem, the character travels to three locations. For example, in one story there is a man who wants to buy a gorilla. First, he goes to the hat factory, but there are no gorillas there. Next he goes to the pizza restaurant, but there are no gorillas there either. Finally, he goes to the Gorillas Are Us store, where there are plenty of gorillas. The man buys a gorilla and takes it home. He is very happy.

According to Ray and Seely (1998), one of the keys to successful language learning is multiple repetitions. TPRS advocates maintain that a student must hear a word 75 times before it is committed to long-term memory. The TPRS methodology achieves these multiple repetitions through a technique called *circling*. As mentioned previously, each story starts out with a problem. In the case of the sample story in which a man wants to buy a gorilla, the TPRS teacher begins the circling technique by asking a series of yes/no questions, such as "Does the man want to buy an elephant?" Next the teacher asks a series of either/or questions, such as "Does the man want to buy a gorilla or an elephant?" Next the teacher asks a series of questions using interrogative words, such as "What does the man want to buy?" When the answer to a question is not evident in the story, students are encouraged to add their own details. The circle of questions is completed with another yes-no question to which students must respond with a complete sentence, rather than a simple "yes" or "no." Through the use of this circling technique students hear the key words of the story multiple times, and details are added to make the story more interesting.

After the details of the story have been established, the students form groups with the same number of people as there are characters in the story. The teacher then retells the story as the students in each group act it out. Next, some of the better students take the teacher's role as narrator, and the acting process is repeated. Finally, smaller groups of two or three students are formed, and students depict the now-familiar story in a series of cartoon panels. Using the pictures as a guide, individual students then take turns retelling the story to the other group members. A variation of this step is to instruct the groups to create a new story and practice telling it in the small group.

As the name implies, the TPRS methodology incorporates reading through the use of extended versions of the stories told in class. The structure of these stories follows the same pattern of having a character with a problem travel to three locations in order to solve it. To guarantee that the input is comprehensible, the first step in the reading process is for the students to translate the story (Ray & Seely, 1998).

The centrality of such stories as the basis for all subsequent language practice is a unique feature of TPRS. "TPR Storytelling is completely planned and methodical. Stories are invented, using specific vocab [*sic*] items/expressions. TPR is wonderful for long term (memory) retention of individual vocab items, and the storytelling helps the learner contextualize the vocab and use it in relevant ways" (Gaab, 1997). Stories have a number of characteristics that make them valuable for education, as Rossiter (2002) points out:

> Stories are effective as educational tools because they are believable, rememberable, and entertaining. The believability stems from the fact that stories deal with human-like experience that we tend to perceive as an authentic and credible source of knowledge. Stories make information more rememberable because they involve us in the actions and intentions of the characters. In so doing, stories invite active meaning making. (Rossiter, 2002, p. 1)

However, many contemporary researchers advocate the use of *authentic* stories. Curtain and Dahlberg (2004) cite the potential of stories to provide integrated practice in a number of skill areas. They recommend stories that are highly predictable, repetitive, and that lend themselves to dramatization and visual representation (p. 63). Lipton (1998) echoes the idea of active participation on the part of the students by saying that the ideal story "should have a short refrain that is repeated periodically throughout the story, so that after a while the children naturally chime in and repeat the refrain without being asked" (p. 129). Wajnryb (1986) recommends stories for teaching second languages because of their appeal to the affective domain and their authentic communicative nature. Nevertheless, TPRS shows a decided preference for teacher-created, non-authentic stories with minimal cultural content. Rather than selecting pre-existing authentic folktales or children's stories from the target culture, the TPRS teacher creates stories that are bizarre, exaggerated, and personalized. For the TPRS teacher, considerations of culture, comparisons, connections, communities, and all other content are secondary to the development of listening comprehension and oral proficiency. In this way proponents of TPRS focus on certain skills and set aside others.

Contemporary Considerations

As mentioned previously, TPRS is most closely related to its namesake, TPR, and the Natural Approach. All three methodologies identify comprehensible input as the primary agent for second language acquisition. All three conceive of successful language learning as primarily an unconscious, intuitive process similar to the way children learn their first language. Finally, all three methodologies emphasize the learning of vocabulary as the most important task facing a learner. Beyond these similarities, TPRS has more in common with older language teaching methodologies than with contemporary, proficiency-based instruction. For example, TPRS's use of repetitive questioning (circle of questions) and limited vocabulary is reminiscent of the Audiolingual Method. Likewise, reliance on question-and-answer exchanges for practice in listening and speaking and the inductive teaching of grammar are closely related to the Direct Method. Finally, TPRS's use of translation of guide words and reading selections is similar to the Grammar Translation method.

Recent research in language acquisition, with its emphasis on the role of the learner and the social and cultural contexts that both affect and are affected by language, has little in common with the behaviorist-influenced ALM and the traditions of GT. This work focuses instead on theories of learning rather than theories of language (Salmani-Nodoushan, 2006). Current research indicates that the learner's personal and institutional biographies are central to language acquisition and use (Hopper, 1998). There is much evidence to indicate that classroom interaction fundamentally shapes the nature of learning tasks and that interaction stimulates not only the linguistic, but also the cognitive and social development of the learners (Brooks & Donato, 1994; Donato, 2000; Hall, 1995; Hall, 1997; Platt & Brooks, 2002; Wells, 1999). Nunan (1999), for example, points out that many definitions of the ability to function in another language center on a learner's ability to speak it, but he adds that there are a number of factors that influence both the teaching and development of this ability. These factors include how the teacher and learners define such issues as competence and the characteristics of different speech events, the background and motivation of the learner, the way that the language course is designed, and the materials and tasks that learners have to support their development (p. 225). TPRS, however, emphasizes the importance of what the teacher says and does, with little mention of how the learner engages in the process.

The emphasis on sociocultural theory in current research places the learner as an active participant in the learning process—a participant who, in fact, can determine the outcome of the process (see, for example, Bloome, et al., 2005; Hall, Hendricks, & Orr, 2004; Vygotsky, 1978). The influence of this theory on research and the subsequent application of this research to classroom practice illustrate the move over the last century from what Salmani-Nodoushan (2006) describes as language-centered methods, those based exclusively on theories of language, to more learner-centered methods that take into consideration the learning process. Shrum and Glisan (2005, p. 68) contrast the roles of the teacher and student and the integration of culture between language-centered and learner-centered methods, using the terms "old paradigm" and "new paradigm" respectively. As researchers, we believe that the old paradigm places the teacher at the center of the instructional process, and learners assume a passive role in the learning process. The new paradigm reverses these roles. In the old paradigm, cultural instruction is limited to bits and pieces of unrelated information interspersed among the more dominant linguistic objectives. In the new paradigm, teachers balance and integrate cultural and linguistic objectives. Ironically, TPRS has more in common with older, language-centered methods than with more recent, learner-centered approaches. The TPRS teacher is the principal creator of language, as well as the audience and evaluator of limited student input. TPRS places little emphasis on cultural objectives, instead relying upon humorous, contrived stories with few, if any, authentic texts.

Contemporary emphasis on the learner's cognitive and social development is also evident in the powerful impact that Backward Design (Wiggins & McTighe, 2005) has had in such areas as teacher education and the development of state foreign language curricula. This concept, which emphasizes the interaction of curriculum, assessment, and instructional design, focuses on "developing and deepening understanding of important ideas" (p. 3). Accordingly, instruction not only teaches skills, but it also guides students in thinking critically about how they choose to apply those skills. As an example, Wiggins and McTighe discuss the difference between reading as a skill that decodes symbols on a page and reading as a process that emphasizes the interaction of a reader with a text (p. 9). Such differentiation is similar to that of the Framework of Communicative Modes, the basis for the *Standards*. This Framework also emphasizes the role of context and the knowledge and skills from which individuals draw in order to participate in an event, be it the interpretation of a poster or the creation of a letter to a friend (National Standards in Foreign Language Education Project, 1999).

An examination of state foreign language curricula further highlights the differences between the tenets of TPRS and trends in foreign language teaching. In Georgia, for instance, teachers who participate in the training for using Georgia's *Modern Language & Latin Standards* (Georgia Department of Education, 2007) learn how to design cohesive unit plans that employ the concepts of Backward Design in the context of the *Standards*. The *South Carolina Academic Standards for Modern and Classical Languages* (2007) emphasize a pedagogical approach that includes open-ended activities that call for higher-order thinking skills and reflection, rather than recollection of factual information, and an active and creative role for teachers and students that permits the creative use of language and negotiated meaning in a variety of situations. These *South Carolina Standards* (2007) also emphasize the importance of taking into consideration diverse learning styles and current research.

One can see that all of these examples stress the necessity of designing instruction according to the needs of the learner rather than according to the tenets of a particular methodology. Furthermore, we have demonstrated that they emphasize the importance of current language-centered research, as opposed to the learner-centered premise of TPRS.

Directions for the Future

As we noted earlier, there is little research to support the effusive claims of increased student motivation and achievement that practitioners of TPRS make;

and there is a similar lack of qualitative data to offer insight into the educational contexts where TPRS is utilized. Moreover, research into the ways that teachers' backgrounds and identities influence their teaching has grown enormously in the past decade (Bailey et al., 1996; Freeman, 1996; Freeman & Richards, 1996). Salmani-Nodoushan (2006) points out that there

> are many observations that reveal that teachers seldom conform to methods which they are supposed to be following; they refuse to be the slaves of methods. In other words, teachers in actual practice often fail to reflect the underlying philosophies of methods which they claim to be following.... Teaching is a dynamic, interactional process in which the teacher's "method" results from the process of interaction between the teacher, the learners, and the instructional tasks and activities over time. (p. 130)

An examination of these interaction processes in a TPRS classroom could reveal much about the characteristics of a successful TPRS classroom. For example, we do not know if teachers use the official TPRS method or if they adapt it for their particular contexts.

There are other teacher-based factors worth examining, as well. For instance, in an era when we see teachers entering the profession through a variety of alternative and traditional preparation routes, does this type of method offer an unambiguous way of dealing with the myriad of stresses that novice teachers face by reducing classroom variability through the manipulation of learner responses and a highly structured approach to presenting new information? We also need to understand the characteristics of learners who flourish with TPRS. For example, do successful TPRS learners exercise particular learning strategies to the exclusion of others?

Conclusions

Those who question the value of TPRS as a methodology do so based on both historical and contemporary considerations. For the TPRS teacher, considerations of culture, comparisons, connections, communities, and all other content are secondary to the development of listening comprehension and oral proficiency. Despite the enthusiastic praise from TPRS teachers, this exclusive emphasis on listening and speaking is a matter of concern for teachers.

> When I say "It works," I mean of course that it works for what it has been created to do: foster language acquisition. But soon after adopting the method, I began asking myself: Sure it works, but is language acquisition the only thing that is supposed to be going on in my classes? Is it enough to get students to understand silly stories in French and be able to tell them back? What about culture and history? Language acquisition is a skill – what about knowledge? (Day, 2006, p. 29)

Such comments are indicative of the ambivalence that many non-TPRS practitioners experience, as well. It is impossible to ignore the enthusiasm expressed by so many teachers in such a wide variety of instructional contexts, and yet the method runs counter to recent research about learners and the nature of language itself.

References

American Council on the Teaching of Foreign Languages. (1982). *Provisional proficiency guidelines.* Hastings-on-Hudson, NY: American Council on the Teaching of Foreign Languages.

Asher, J. (2007). How to apply TPRS for best results. Retrieved November 26, 2007, from http://www.tpr-world.com/tpr-storytelling.html

Asher, J. J. (1969). The total physical response approach to second language learning. *Modern Language Journal, 53*, 3-17.

Bachman, L. F. (1990). *Fundamental considerations in language testing.* Oxford, England: Oxford University Press.

Bailey, K. M., Bergthold, B., Braunstein, B., Fleischman, N. J., Holbrook, M. P., Truman, J., Waissbluth, X., & Zambo, L. J. (1996). The language learner's autobiography: Examining the apprenticeship of observation. In D. Freeman & J.C. Richards (Eds.), *Teacher learning in language teaching* (pp. 11-29). Edinburgh, Scotland: Cambridge University.

Baird, J. (1997). Re: TPRS video. *Foreign language teaching forum.* Retrieved November 30, 2007, from http://listserv.buffalo.edu/cgi-bin/ wa?A2=ind9703&L=flteach&T=0&X=22EBE41CF2796DDBA1&Y=aguas53%40gmail.com&P=2483

Bloome, D., Carter, S. P., Christian, B. M., Otto, S., & Shuart-Faris, N. (2005). *Discourse analysis and the study of classroom language and literacy events: A microethnographic perspective.* Mahwah, NJ: Lawrence Erlbaum.

Brooks, F. B., & Donato, R. (1994). Vygotskyan approaches to understanding foreign language learner discourse during communicative tasks. *Hispania, 77*, 262-272.

Brown, H. D. (1994). *Teaching by principles: An interactive approach to language pedagogy.* Upper Saddle River, NJ: Prentice Hall Regents.

Celce-Murcia, M., Zoltan, D., & Thurrell, S. (1995). Communicative competence: A pedagogically motivated model with content specification. *Issues in Applied Linguistics, 6*, 5-35.

Curtain, H. A., & Dahlberg, C. A. (2004). *Languages and children: Making the match.* Boston: Pearson Education.

Day, R. (2006). TPRS: What is it and is it for you? *Language Educator, 1,* 28-30.

Donato, R. (2000). Sociocultural contributions to understanding the foreign and second language classroom. In J. P. Lantolf (Ed.), *Sociocultural theory and second language learning* (pp. 27-50). Oxford, England: Oxford University

Freeman, D. (1996). Renaming experience/reconstructing practice: Developing new understandings of teaching. In D. Freeman & J. C. Richards (Eds.), *Teacher learning in language teaching* (pp. 221-240). Edinburgh, Scotland: Cambridge University.

Freeman, D., & Richards, J. C. (Eds.). (1996). *Teacher learning in language teaching*. Edinburgh, Scotland: Cambridge University.

Gaab, C. (1997). Re: TPR storytelling-re-telling stories. Foreign language teaching forum. Retrieved November 30, 2007, from http://listserv.buffalo.edu/cgi-bin/wa?A2=ind9704&L=FLTEACH&P=R13166&I=-3

Georgia Department of Education. (2007). *Modern language & Latin standards.* Retrieved November 26, 2007, from http://www.georgiastandards.org/language.aspx

Hall, J. K. (1995). "Aw, man, where you goin'?": Classroom interaction and the development of L2 interactional competence. *Issues in Applied Linguistics, 6,* 37-62.

Hall, J. K. (1997). A consideration of SLA as a theory of practice. *Modern Language Journal, 81*, 301-306.

Hall, J. K., Hendricks, S., & Orr, J. L. (2004). Dialogues in the "global village": NNS/NS collaboration in classroom interaction. *Critical Inquiry in Language Studies: An International Journal, 1*, 63-88.

Hopper, P. J. (1998). Emergent grammar. In M. Tomasello (Ed.), *The new psychology of language: Cognitive and functional approaches to language structure* (pp. 155-175). Mahwah, NJ: Lawrence Erlbaum.

Krashen, S. D., & Terrell, T. D. (1983). *The natural approach: Language acquisition in the classroom.* Hayward, CA: Alemany Press.

Lipton, G. (1998). *Practical handbook to elementary foreign language programs.* Lincolnwood, IL: National Textbook.

National Standards in Foreign Language Education Project. (1999). *Standards for foreign language learning in the 21st century.* Yonkers, NY: Author.

Nunan, D. (1999). *Second language teaching and learning.* Boston: Heinle and Heinle.

Nunan, D. (2005). Classroom research. In E. Hinkel (Ed.), *Handbook of research in second language teaching and learning* (pp. 225-240). Mahwah, NJ: Lawrence Erlbaum.

Omaggio Hadley, A. (2001). *Teaching language in context.* Boston: Heinle & Heinle

Platt, E., & Brooks, F. B. (2002). Task engagement: A turning point in foreign language development. *Language Learning, 52*, 365-400.

Ray, B., & Seely, C. (1998). *Fluency through TPR storytelling.* Berkeley, CA: Command Performance Language Institute.

Richards, J. C., & Rodgers, T. (1986). *Approaches and methods in language teaching.* Cambridge, UK: University Press.

Rossiter, M. (2002). *Narrative and stories in adult teaching and learning.* (Report No. EDO-CE-02-241). Washington, DC: Education Resources Information Center. (ERIC Document Reproduction Service No. ED346082)

Salmani-Nodoushan, M. A. (2006). Language teaching: State of the art. *The Reading Matrix, 6,* 125-140.

Shrum, J. L., & Glisan, E. (2005). *Teacher's handbook: Contextualized language instruction* (3rd ed.). Boston: Thomson Heinle.

South Carolina academic standards for modern and classical languages. Retrieved November 26, 2007, from http://ed.sc.gov/agency/offices/cso/document ModernClassicalLanguages2006.pdf

Steele, S. (1997). Re: TPRStorytelling. Foreign Language Teaching Forum. Retrieved November 29, 2007, from http://listserv.buffalo.edu/cgi-bin/ wa?A2= ind 9709&L=FLTEACH&P=R31392&D=0&H=0&I=3&O=T&T=0&X=5A79 FB4069CA38B4FF&Y=aguas53%40gmail.com

Swain, M. (1985). Communicative competence: Some roles of comprehensible input and comprehensive output in its development. In S. Gass & C. Madden (Eds.), *Input in second language acquisition* (pp. 235-256). Rowley, MA: Newbury House.

Terrell, T. D. (1986). Acquisition in the natural approach: The binding/access framework. *Modern Language Journal, 70,* 213-227.

Vygotsky, L. (1978). *Mind in society.* Cambridge, MA: Harvard University.

Wajnryb, R. (1986). Storytelling and language learning. *Babel, 21,* 17-24.

Wells, G. (1999). *Dialogic inquiry: Toward a sociocultural practice and theory of education.* Cambridge, UK: Cambridge University.

Wiggins, G., & McTighe, J. (2005). *Understanding by design* (2nd ed.). Alexandria, VA: Association for Supervision and Curriculum Development.

3

Technoconstructivism and the Millennial Generation: Creative Writing in the Foreign Language Classroom

Edwina Spodark
Hollins University

Abstract

The Millennial Generation is different from the generations of foreign language students who have preceded them. In the classroom, Millennial students prefer collaborative learning, the use of technology, a peer review/support/connection, structure, hands-on learning, and opportunities for personal creativity. This contemporary generation needs teachers to adopt a more relevant methodology to reflect their understanding of and respect for the information mindset that students bring to the classroom. Given these traits, the most effective methodology for their learning environment is one that blends the pedagogical practices advocated by social constructivism with the benefits of educational technology that speaks directly to the learning styles of Millennial Generation students: technoconstructivism. This style of teaching effectively engages Millennial Generation students in creative writing in the target language by incorporating assignments such as Web-based pre-writing activities, computerized multiple-draft assignments, peer reviews, and individual multimedia presentations.

Background

Simultaneously referred to as the Net Generation, Gen(eration) M, Generation Y, Echo-Boomers, and the Nintendo Generation (Carlson, 2005; Howe, 2005; McGlynn, 2005; Oblinger & Oblinger, 2005; Schooley, 2005; Tapscott, 1998; Tucker, 2006), students from the Millennial generation are making their way through classrooms across the country and are impacting the educational environment along the way. In their book *Millennials Rising*, Howe and Strauss (2000) first delineated as the Millennial Generation those "born in or after 1982 [and constituting] the much touted high school Class of 2000" (p. 4). This definition later gave rise to an expanded classification as "anyone born around the time the PC was introduced" (Oblinger & Oblinger, 2005, p. 22). Estimates of the size of the Millennial cohort in the United States vary upwards to 100 million, roughly 30% of the population and approximately 33 percent larger than the Baby Boomers. Chief among their attributes are a penchant for collaborative learning, expectations for peer review and support, the need for structure, hands-on learning, the use of technology in the classroom, and opportunities for personal creativity. Breeding (2006) observes that Millennial students prefer to gather in groups and rarely work on projects or study alone. A direct outgrowth is the popularity of support and social networking sites such as MySpace.com, YouTube.com, Digg.com, and Facebook.com. Today's students rely on peer reviews of everything from homework assignments to opinions on music. Howe and Strauss note that Millennial college students "learn in groups, deliver presentations in groups, and get graded in groups. They review each other's assignments and supervise each other's behavior" (2003, p. 93). The collaborative, team-oriented tendency of this high-achieving generation leads to a strong desire for structure and feedback in classroom assignments, with demands to know the precise criteria for success. Therefore, given their unique characteristics and size, this group will trigger change as it passes through the educational system, and foreign languages teachers need to adapt their teaching methods accordingly.

These learning style preferences are the understandable consequence of the transition to a constructivist methodology during the formative years of the Millennial Generation. They are more kinesthetic than any group before them, and as students of the information age mindset, they prefer doing rather than knowing (Frand, 2000).

> Constructionism argues that people learn best by *doing* rather than simply being told, and the enthusiasm youngsters have for a fact or concept they "discovered" on their own is much more likely to be meaningful and retained than the same fact simply written out on the teacher's blackboard. (Tapscott, 1998, p. 144)

Among the most prominent of these changes necessary is the integration of technology into the classroom, and Millennial students "literally demand interactivity as they construct knowledge" (Schooley, 2005, p. 1). While comfortable with technology, they seem to appreciate structured activities that permit creativity, and they want to be involved with real-life issues that matter to them.

Given the propensity of Millennial Generation students for collaborative learning and peer review, their need for structure and hands-on learning, their proficiency in the use of technology, and their need for personal creativity, the most appropriate and effective pedagogical methodology to ensure their success is technoconstructivism, a "blending of the pedagogical practices advocated by social constructivism with the benefits of educational technology" (Spodark, 2005, p. 429). Noon (1998-1999, 1999) defines technoconstructivism by comparing it with electronic traditionalism. Teachers who are electronic traditionalists use technology in the classroom, but in very traditional ways. For them the computer is an electronic encyclopedia for simple research or an AV tool to show Web pages instead of videotapes, and e-mail is simply a supplement to pencil-and-paper writing activities. On the other hand, teachers who are technoconstructivists use technology to access primary sources. They place technology in the hands of their students and allow them to choose the most appropriate technology for answering their questions or for communicating with others. In dynamic classrooms of technoconstructivists, teachers control curriculum and assessment, but students, with appropriate guidance from the teacher, control learning by participating in making decisions about *what* they will learn and *how* they will learn it (Noon, 1999). In this type of dynamic classroom environment, Millennial students thrive.

Technoconstructivism in the Foreign Language Classroom

One ideal example of a technoconstructivist approach in the foreign language classroom is a course called *Stories and Legends* taught during a fifth-semester university French class. Students explore the rich history of francophone stories and legends and engage in the creations of their own. In class they learn about and discuss the differences in archetypes of story and legend genres. The students discover, among other things, how the five senses can form the organizing principle of a story, how animals act as symbols and metaphors to drive home meaning, and how humor plays a role in the lessons taught. They learn about the origins and role of the national legend, how legends of different francophone regions vary, and why they remain important to this day. In addition to this traditional approach to the subject, the students are also asked to analyze the structure and power of stories and legends from their own generation. The class views the film short by Philippe Orreindy (2004), *J'attendrai le suivant* (I'll Take the Next One), a remarkable video available on the popular Web site YouTube at <http://www.youtube.com/watch?v=Bom0uI0n-1Q>. It was the winner of the Prix du Court Métrage at the European Film Awards in 2004 and was nominated for Live Action Short Film at the Academy Awards in 2003 and at the Cannes Film Festival in 2004. This direct appeal to the Millennial Generation via computer technology provides a bridge to the creative portion of the course and uses technoconstructivist principles to guide Millennial students through the process of creative writing by taking into account their particular traits, learning preferences, and needs.

Students then begin to write their own stories in French. The first step is a prewriting activity that involves students with a composition topic by reflecting upon what might be included in their papers, helping them work out rhetorical problems, and reviewing or providing useful vocabulary (Barnett, 1989). In this case, however, the prewriting activity is a Web-based exercise that asks students to discover the francophone world, explore Web sites about specific francophone countries, and locate additional Web sites that describe those countries (Appendix A). This activity allows the students to explore their possibilities and think about what elements they might adopt for their narratives before they actually start composing. Drawing upon the Millennial Generation's partiality towards collaboration, this intentional, hands-on activity does not end when students e-mail their assignments to the instructor. At that point, all of the Web sites, the ones provided in the assignment as well as those contributed by the students, are organized into a Web page of authentic francophone resources complete with country-specific images and comments about the content and usefulness of each site. This community-constructed Web page is then posted on the class Blackboard site under Course Information for all to use.

Knowing Millennial students' needs for careful planning, unambiguous directions, and step-by-step instructions, teachers need to provide a clear set of guidelines and directions. Students are told specifically how to name e-mail attachments, who receives their work, and the precise deadlines. Students in the *Stories and Legends* course complete a preliminary outline of their stories (Appendix B), an online assignment that includes their choice of francophone country, elements of the country that provide an appropriate setting for their stories, well-developed descriptions of their main characters, an outline of their plot, and the first draft of the first paragraph (Appendix C). They are then directed to e-mail their work to all the other members of the class, including the teacher. The template for the preliminary outline contains the format for peer review of each student's work, a place for an overall evaluation, and space to provide up to five suggestions for improvement. This process lets students know the importance of peer review in the foreign language writing process and says,

> The class is a team. We all have a stake in each other's progress. We are embarked on the project of improving writing together. Editing texts together is a mutually supportive and instructive activity. All benefit. All contribute. (Gaudiani, 1981, p. 10)

Each student is asked to critique the work of every other student in the class and to e-mail each individual the results of the analysis. This feedback provides authors with several evaluations of their work and a number of suggestions for improvement. At the same time that it increases self-awareness of problems and possibilities, the peer-review process encourages spontaneous and collaborative work among students (Burns & Brien, 2003). At this point, the teacher gives specific feedback on the organization, character development, and integration of francophone elements in individual stories.

After students reflect on the advice they receive from the other members of the class, they prepare a first draft of their stories, with very clear directions for this portion of the assignment (Appendix D). The template for the first draft replicates the preliminary outline form, with the added requirement that students then write three paragraphs for each of the sections of their original outlines (Appendix E). Like the preliminary outline exercise, this draft of their stories will be evaluated by the rest of the class using the same online process as before, and students receive feedback on their writing and story ideas. At this point, the teacher comments on any grammatical problems, being careful to avoid giving the impression that grammar is more important than the message students are attempting to convey. Students are instructed to access the class Blackboard site for PowerPoint grammar review lessons developed by the teacher for assistance in revising their texts. They e-mail the revised copies to the professor as many times as needed to correct problem areas in their texts. This phase is followed by individual meetings between each student and the teacher to discuss any other grammatical problems and to receive one final overall evaluation of the story by the professor. Students are also reminded that they will present their stories to the class, and a list of suggested presentation modes is posted on the class Blackboard site (Appendix F). The professor discusses the method of class presentation that the student is planning and resolves any questions about the presentation process.

The presentation of the narratives is the concluding step and the highlight of the semester. Students take great pride in presenting their work to the audience of their peers, all of whom have collaborated on the project. Each presentation is a hands-on creation that illustrates the students' stories in a personal and individual way. Occasionally, presentations are uploaded to the class Web site for viewing by family and friends. This active, intentional, collaborative approach to developing a technology-based creative writing project for Millennial Generation students fosters a sense of collective ownership and interest in the creative process of each story under construction. It also allows students to share their creations beyond the classroom environment, much as they share their daily lives on MySpace, Facebook, and blogs.

Conclusions

As Frand (2000) observes, "over the next few years these students will become the majority, spreading like a tidal wave across higher education and demanding changes in the way we operate" (p. 16). In looking at Millennials' distinct learning preferences, Oblinger and Oblinger (2005) and Raines (2003) conclude that these students appreciate teamwork, experiential activities, structure, and the use of technology. In addition, their penchant for staying connected to their peer groups by using technology will inevitably compel change in their learning environments. For this generation the best learning model is "one of student-centered discovery enabled by emerging technologies" (Tapscott, 1998, p. 155). As demonstrated in this account of a foreign language writing project, technoconstructivism takes into account Millennial students' affinity for collaborative learning, peer review and support, structure, hands-on learning, the use of technology, and opportunities for personal creativity. This technology-enhanced pedagogy speaks directly to Millennials' learning styles, preferences, and habits and provides educators with the best method for reaching the hearts and minds of the students they teach.

References

Barnett, M. A. (1989). Writing as a process. *French Review, 63,* 31-44.
Breeding, M. (2006). Technology for the next generation. *Computers in Libraries, 26,* 28-30.
Burns, A., & Brien, D. L. (2003). Teaching electronic creative writing. *Issues in Writing, 13,* 158-187.
Carlson, S. (2005, October 7). The net generation goes to college. *Chronicle of Higher Education, 52,* A34.

Frand, J. L. (2000, September/October). The information-age mindset: Changes in students and implications for higher education. *EDUCAUSE Review, 35,* 15-24.

Gaudiani, C. (1981). *Teaching writing in the foreign language curriculum.* Language in education: Theory and practice, vol. 43. Washington, DC: Center for Applied Linguistics.

Howe, N. (2005, September 1). Harnessing the power of Millennials: New strategies for a confident, achieving youth generation. *School Administrator, 62,* 18-22.

Howe, N., & Strauss, W. (2000). *Millennials rising: The next great generation* New York: Vintage Books.

Howe, N., & Strauss, W. (2003). *Millennials go to college: Strategies for a new generation on campus: Recruiting and admissions, campus life, and the classroom.* Washington DC: American Association of Collegiate Registrars and Admissions Officers (AACRAO) and LifeCourse Associates.

McGlynn, A. P. (2005). Teaching Millennials, our newest cultural cohort. *Education Digest, 71,* 12-16.

Noon, S. (1998, December, 1999, January). 4 stages of technology adoption: Part three: The electronic traditionalist. *Classroom Connect Newsletter: The K-12 Educators' Guide to the Internet, 5,* 21.

Noon, S. (1999, February). 4 stages of technology adoption: Part four: Training technoconstructivists. *Classroom Connect Newsletter: The K-12 Educators' Guide to the Internet, 5,* 11.

Oblinger, D. G., & Oblinger, J. L. (2005). *Educating the net generation.* EDUCAUSE. Retrieved November 27, 2007, from http://www.educause.edu/educatingthenetgen/

Orreindy, P. (Director). (2004). *J'attendrai le suivant* [Film Short]. Retrieved November 27, 2007, from http://www.youtube.com/watch?v=Bom0uI0n-1Q

Raines, C. (2003). *Connecting generations: The sourcebook for a new workplace.* Menlo Park, CA: Crisp Publications.

Schooley, C. (2005, September 20). Get ready: The Millennials are coming! Forrester Research. Retrieved November 27, 2007, from http://www.aaa.biz/aaacampus articles/articles/millennials.pdf

Spodark, E. (2005). Technoconstructivism for the undergraduate foreign language classroom. *Foreign Language Annals, 38,* 428-435.

Tapscott, D. (1998). *Growing up digital: The rise of the net generation.* New York: McGraw Hill.

Tucker, P. (2006, May-June). Teaching the Millennial Generation. *The Futurist, 40,* 7.

Appendix A

Exercice de web #1

1. Allez au site web suivant: [Go to the following Web site:]
    Cartes du monde francophone [Maps of the francophone world]
    http://a.ttfr.free.fr/dossiers.php?dossier=francophonie

    Notez cinq pays francophones qui vous intéressent. Indiquez aussi dans quelle partie du monde chaque pays se trouve: [Note five francophone countries that interest you. Indicate as well in what part of the world they are located:]

2. Allez aux sites web indiqués pour les cinq pays francophones suivants et notez cinq faits culturels intéressants. Puis trouvez un autre site web intéressant que vous recommanderiez aux autres pour chaque pays de la liste. [For the following five francophone countries, go to the indicated Web sites and note five interesting cultural facts about each one. Then find another interesting Web site that you would recommend to others for each country on the list.]

    A. Québec
        http://www.gouv.qc.ca/
        http://www.toile.qc.ca/
        Faits: 1.   2.   3.   4.   5.
        Autre Site Web: _____

    B. Vietnam
        http://www.cap-vietnam.com/
        http://www.ambafrance-vn.org/
        Faits: 1.   2.   3.   4.   5.
        Autre Site Web: _____

    C. Sénégal
        http://www.gouv.sn/
        http://www.senegal-online.com/
        Faits: 1.   2.   3.   4.   5.
        Autre Site Web: _____

    D. Maroc
        http://www.ambafrance-ma.org/
        http://www.tourisme-marocain.com/Onmt_FR/Marches/INS/index.aspx
        Faits:1.   2.   3.   4.   5.
        Autre Site Web: _____

    E. Haïti
        http://www.alliance-haiti.com/
        http://haiti-reference.com/
        Faits: 1.   2.   3.   4.   5.
        Autre Site Web: _____

Appendix B

Conte: Travail de préparation [Story: Preparation work]

Renseignements: [Directions]

Téléchargez l'esquisse préliminaire de votre conte à partir de notre site dans Blackboard (utilisez "SAVE AS"). Appelez-la "CONTE1 + vos initiales". Exemple: CONTE1ES (ES initiales du professeur). Complétez-la et distribuez-la à toute la classe (y compris le professeur) par "send e-mail, all users, add attachment" sur notre site Blackboard avant dix heures et demie du matin le mardi 20 février. Le sujet du courriel doit être: TRAVAIL DE + votre nom. Chaque personne doit lire attentivement l'esquisse de tous les autres étudiants de la classe. Ensuite ajoutez votre nom à la liste à la fin de l'esquisse et écrivez une évaluation honnête du travail de votre camarade de classe et faites-lui 2-3 suggestions utiles pour améliorer son conte. Sauvez votre version avec vos commentaires en ajoutant vos initiales au nom original. Exemple: CONTE1ESYY (si YY a fait l'évaluation). Envoyez vos commentaires avant huit heures et demie du matin le jeudi 22 février avec le sujet du courriel: EVALUATION DE + votre nom. MAIS n'envoyez vos commentaires qu'à la personne qui a complété l'esquisse et au professeur (PAS à TOUTE la classe – choisissez "e-mail, select users, add attachment"). Quand vous recevrez tous les commentaires des autres étudiants, lisez-les attentivement et incorporez des changements qui sont, à votre avis, des améliorations dans le texte de votre conte. La prochaine étape sera d'écrire des paragraphes pour toutes les parties de votre esquisse. Pensez aussi à comment vous voulez présenter votre conte à la classe. Il y a une liste de suggestions sur notre site dans Blackboard sous "Course Information."

[Download the preliminary outline for your story from our Blackboard site (use "SAVE AS"). Call it "STORY1 + your initials." Example: STORY1ES. Complete the story and circulate it to everyone in the class (including the teacher), using "send e-mail, all users, add attachment" on our Blackboard site by 10:30 a.m., Tuesday, February 20. The subject of the e-mail should be: WORK FROM + your name. Carefully read the outline from all the other students in the class, then add your name to the list at the end of the outline, write an honest evaluation of your classmate's work, and give 2-3 useful suggestions for improving the story. Save your version and your comments by adding your initials to the original name. Example: STORY1ESYY (if YY did the evaluation). Send your comments before 8:30 a.m., Thursday, February 22, with the e-mail subject line: EVALUATION BY + your name. Send your comments only to the person who completed the outline and to the teacher, not to the entire class. (Choose "e-mail, select users, add attachment.") When you receive all the comments from the other students, read them carefully and incorporate any changes that are, in your opinion, improvements to the text of your story. The next step will be to write portions of a paragraph for each section in your outline. Think about how you would like to present your story to the class. There is a list of presentation modes on our Blackboard site under "Course Information" as suggestions to help you decide.]

Appendix C

Conte: Esquisse préliminaire [Story: Preliminary outline]

Complétez cette esquisse et envoyez-la à toute la classe. [Complete this outline and send it to the class.]

A. Mise en scène

>   Dans quel pays francophone (PAS LA FRANCE) voulez-vous que votre conte ait lieu? (Si vous voulez, vous pouvez consulter notre site dans Blackboard où vous trouverez une liste de tous les sites web de notre exercice sur les pays francophones y compris les suggestions de vos camarades de classe et des sites d'autres pays francophones trouvés par le professeur.) [In which francophone country (not France) do you want your story to take place? You can consult our Blackboard site for a list of Web sites compiled by your classmates and the teacher related to francophone countries.]

>   Dressez une liste de 5 faits intéressants que vous pouvez utiliser dans votre conte pour lui donner l'atmosphère du pays francophone que vous avez choisi ci-dessus. [Make a list of 5 interesting facts that you can use in your story to give it an ambiance of the francophone country you chose.]

B. Personnages [Characters]

>   Dressez une liste d'au moins 5 personnages qui feront partie de votre conte. Faites une description de chacun d'entre eux. [Make a list of at least 5 characters who will be part of your story. Give a description of each one.]

C. Intrigue [Plot]

>   Esquissez les étapes de l'intrigue de votre conte. [Outline the plot of your story.]
>   I. Introduction
>   II. ? . . . .
>   . . . .
>   IX. Dénouement
>   X. Conclusion ? (exemple: conte africain = la morale)

D. Le premier paragraphe [The first paragraph]

Ecrivez le premier paragraphe de votre conte [Write the first paragraph of your story]

Travail d'évaluation et de suggestions [Evaluation and suggestions]

Nom de l'étudiant qui critique le travail [Name of student critiquing the work]

Evaluation honnête du travail [Honest evaluation of the work]

Suggestions:

Appendix D

Conte: Première esquisse [Story: First draft]

Renseignements: [Directions :]

    Téléchargez la première esquisse de votre conte dans notre site Blackboard (utilisez "SAVE AS"). Appelez-la "CONTE2 + vos initiales". Exemple: CONTE2ES (ES initiales du professeur). Remplissez-la et distribuez-la à toute la classe (y compris le professeur) par "send e-mail, all users, add attachment" sur notre site dans Blackboard d'ici neuf heures du matin le mardi 11 mars. Le sujet du courriel doit être: TRAVAIL2 DE + votre nom. Chaque personne doit lire attentivement les paragraphes des contes de tous les autres étudiants de la classe. Ajoutez votre nom à la liste à la fin de l'esquisse et écrivez une évaluation honnête du travail de votre camarade de classe et faites-lui 2-3 suggestions utiles pour améliorer son conte. Sauvez votre version avec vos commentaires en ajoutant vos initiales au nom original. Exemple: CONTE2ESYY (si YY a fait l'évaluation). Envoyez vos commentaires au plus tard à midi le vendredi 14 mars avec le sujet du courriel: EVALUATION2 de + votre nom. MAIS n'envoyez vos commentaires qu'à la personne qui a rempli l'esquisse et au professeur (PAS à TOUTE la classe – choisissez "e-mail, select users, add attachment"). Quand vous recevrez tous les commentaires des autres étudiants, lisez-les attentivement et incorporez des changements qui sont, à votre avis, des améliorations dans le texte de votre conte. La prochaine étape sera de finir le conte et de décider comment vous voulez présenter votre conte à la classe. Il y a une liste de suggestions dans notre site Blackboard sous "Course Information." Les présentations auront lieu le jeudi 29 mars.

    [Download the first draft for your story from our Blackboard site, using "SAVE AS". Call it "STORY2 + your initials." Example: STORY2ES (ES the teacher's initials). Complete the story and circulate it to everyone in the class, including the teacher, by 9:00 a.m., Tuesday, March 11. Use "send e-mail, all users, add attachment" on our Blackboard site. The subject of the e-mail should be: WORK2 FROM + your name. Carefully read the paragraphs from all the other students in the class, then add your name to the list at the end of the outline, write an honest evaluation of your classmate's work, and give 2-3 useful suggestions for improving the story. Save your version and your comments by adding your initials to the original name. Example: STORY2ESYY (if YY did the evaluation). Send your comments before noon, Friday, March 14, with the e-mail subject line: EVALUATION2 BY + your name. Send your comments only to the person who completed the draft and to the teacher, not to the entire class. Choose "e-mail, select users, add attachment." When you receive all the comments from the other students, read them carefully and incorporate any changes that are, in your opinion, improvements to the text of your story. The next step will be to complete the story and decide how you want to present your story to the class. There is a list of presentation modes on our Blackboard site under "Course Information" as suggestions to help you decide. Presentations will take place on Thursday, March 29.]

Appendix E

Conte: Première esquisse [Story: First draft]

I. Reproduire l'esquisse des étapes de l'intrigue de votre conte: [Reproduce the outline of the plot of your story:]

    I. Introduction
    II. ?....
    ....
    IX. Dénouement
    X. Conclusion? (exemple: conte africain=la morale)

II. Ecrivez au moins 3 paragraphes pour chacune des parties de votre conte: [Write at least three paragraphs for each section of your story:]

  A. Introduction (y compris le premier paragraphe que vous avez déjà écrit, la mise en scène, l'introduction des personnages et des éléments spécifiques au pays francophone où le conte a lieu). [Introduction (including the first paragraph that you already wrote, the setting, the introduction of characters, and the elements specific to the francophone country where the story takes place)].

Travail d'évaluation et de suggestions [Evaluation work and suggestions]

Nom de l'étudiant qui critique le travail [Name of student writing the critique]

Evaluation honnête du travail [Honest evaluation of the work]

Suggestions:

Appendix F

List of possible presentation modes for stories and legends

1. an illustrated Web page: with original drawings, original pictures that have been scanned, pictures taken from the Internet (properly referenced), or clip art
2. a play
3. a PowerPoint presentation
4. a narrated story using Photo Story or Movie Maker
5. story boards
6. an image-enhanced podcast
7. an illuminated manuscript (handwritten or word processed)
8. a video
9. a song
10. shadow boxes
11. a comic strip
12. a poem
13. a puppet show
14. a music video
15. a fictional blog
16. an illustrated newspaper or magazine article
17. an illustrated game

4

Technology for Oral Assessment

Patricia Early
Peter B. Swanson
Georgia State University

Abstract:

With recent developments in multimedia recording, researchers have begun to investigate the use of technology in oral proficiency assessment. This article addresses the benefits and ease of using seven different multimedia tools to assess P-16 students' oral language proficiency and compares traditional methods of in-class oral language assessment to out-of-class recordings. Additionally, the authors discuss the potential benefits of using technology to lower students' affective filter, to provide teachers with a digital portfolio of student progress, and to increase instructional and preparation time.

Second language instruction in the communicative classroom has as its core a dedication to the ideals, if not the practice, of developing second-language proficiency in four areas: written language, reading proficiency, listening ability, and oral language production (National Standards in Foreign Language Education Project, 1999). The first three areas are the most readily measurable through common assessment instruments, such as written exams. The assessment of oral language production, however, has consistently presented numerous challenges, including the development of useful and flexible rubrics (Foster, Tonkyn, & Wigglesworth, 2000) and the time expended in individual learner assessment (Flewelling, 2002).

Furthermore, unlike written assessments, traditional oral assessments conducted in the classroom rarely leave an assessment artifact that can be archived or easily compared between subjects to measure similarities or differences in learner progress towards proficiency goals. In order to address these concerns, the language laboratories of previous decades are being replaced or refitted to accommodate digital recordings that can facilitate whole-class concurrent, archival recordings (Flewelling, 2002). Presently, researchers are beginning to investigate the uses of emerging technologies and their potential uses within the context of oral proficiency and assessment (Chan, 2003; Egan, 1999; Egbert, 1999; Volle, 2005).

Advances in personal digital technology and developments in hardware and software can supplement or even replace traditional language laboratories. Oral proficiency assessment capabilities are enhanced through the use of digital oral production artifacts and out-of-class recording tasks. This article outlines the functionality, challenges, and advantages of three distinct categories of digital tools and discusses how each was used by undergraduate foreign language students at a southern university. The article concludes with a discussion of the research and the implications of using digital technology for oral language assessment.

Hardware and Software Resources

Software

Although application software exists in many forms and environments, for the purposes of this article, software is defined as an executable computer application that is installed directly on an individual workstation. Dozens of shareware and freeware digital recording programs are available for download. Each has its own interface and features, capable of recording oral production in one or more common recording file formats, WAV and MP3. Basic information regarding these file types is available at <http://en.wikipedia.org/wiki/Audio_file_formats> (Audio file format, 2007). Special measures should be taken to ensure that students' personal computers are kept free of adware, spyware, or license limitations and that the tool required for making recordings will not monopolize computer processing and storage resources. The free *Audacity* recorder (Mazzoni & Dannenberg, 2000), available at <http://audacity.sourceforge.net/>, is an open-source recorder, available to the public with relaxed or non-existent intellectual property restrictions. It is easy to use, yet allows for relatively sophisticated editing capabilities. Sound files are recorded in the WAV format, and an additional *LAME* encoder can be easily downloaded and installed from an associated Web site if MP3 recording is required.

Every computer that utilizes the Windows operating system comes already equipped with the *Windows Sound Recorder*. This program is accessible via the Start Menu by clicking on *Programs > Accessories > Entertainment > Sound Recorder*. The only file format available with the Sound Recorder is the WAV format, but the limited functionality of the recorder is offset by its ease of use.

Webware

Webware encompasses online applications of software that do not require downloads or installation of software on individual computers. These tools are available from any Web-enabled computer. As they are not dependent upon a particular computer operating system, they are accessible to all platforms: Windows, Apple, and Linux. A popular, free Web resource for voice recording and immediate podcasting is *Odeo* (Arturo & Rupert, 2006),available at <www.odeo.com> Once a user account is created by the instructor, a button can be placed on the instructor's website by copying a line of HTML text and pasting it on a class Web site. By clicking on this button, students can record their voices, and the recording can be sent directly to a designated e-mail address. As audio files can be quite large, instructors may wish to create a separate e-mail account that allows for large file storage. An additional Web tool for voice recording is *YackPack* (Fogg, 2005). Educators can download a free version at <www.yackpack.net> or enroll in subscription services at <www.yackpack.com>. Instructors can use this software to establish class "packs," or groups of students, and then interact asynchronously with the students. Prompts and responses can be recorded via the online interface and delivered to either an individual or the entire class, and ongoing discussion threads can be created to share information and facilitate truly communicative exchanges. One disadvantage of *YackPack* is that teachers would need to create a "pack" for each class, and then invite the students to join the pack via e-mail accounts. Students would need to have an active e-mail account prior to joining the class pack. For optimal results, instructors may want to set up the initial accounts in a language lab environment, where media specialists can assist students with the process of establishing accounts and joining groups. Once the initial setup has been completed, recording and submitting files is intuitive, and the interface is easily accessed and utilized.

Portable Hardware

With the widespread diffusion of digital music technology, the prices for personal, portable devices have fallen within a comfortable range for educational purchases. Although the large capacity iPods are still among the digital elite, it is possible to find MP3 recorders with built-in microphones for prices ranging between $35 and $120, depending upon the features and the storage size of the unit. An instructor could use this device to issue a written prompt to the class or prerecord an audio prompt, then check out units to all students, who would then record their responses outside of class. The students would then return the devices to the instructor, who could either offload the recordings onto a master archive or evaluate the recordings at a later time.

The lowest-priced unit investigated was the *Phillips SA1210*, a basic 1GB MP3 player and voice recorder with push-button recording and an integrated microphone. Although the quality of the recording had a distinctly mechanical tone, the articulation was clear and comprehensible. The moderately priced *Creative Zen V* also has 1GB of storage, an integrated microphone, and superior recording quality. This device not only allows the instructor to transfer an audio prompt to the students via a prerecorded message stored on the player, but also to deliver images as prompts, by transferring digital images to the player and having them called up by the student.

The *Sanako* MP3 recorder, designed specifically to serve the needs of language learners and teachers, falls into the upper end of the price range. It comes equipped with only 512 mg of storage capacity, but it has a dual-track recording system, in which students can record their voices while concurrently listening to a teacher track. This feature expands possibilities for question-and-answer assessments or simulated, asynchronous interviews. Although the recording quality was excellent, the recording process was not intuitive and would require a significant amount of training or detailed user guides.

The tools mentioned above are a sample of technology that is affordable, readily available, and simple to implement in language classrooms. In the next section, the researchers discuss a study that was conducted at a large research university, following the selection and implementation of a technology tool. The findings are part of a larger study that sought to identify students' and instructors' perceptions comparing traditional and technology-enhanced oral language assessment.

Method

Procedure

Researchers at a large research university studied 128 students enrolled in first- and second-semester Spanish (n=61) and Japanese (n=67) courses during the 2006-07 academic year. The research sample included both traditional and non-traditional undergraduate students, who ranged in age from 18 to 52 years of age (M=23). Females outnumbered males almost two to one, and there was an almost even distribution of Caucasian (34%), African American (32%), and Hispanic/Asian (34%) students. Most students (88%) reported having studied foreign languages previously in secondary schools.

Students who are enrolled in first- and second-semester Spanish courses have a minimum of two oral language assessments (OLA) during the semester, one at the third week and another at the thirteenth week of the semester. Instructors may assess individual student ability in class, or they may ask students to go to the language laboratory to digitally record responses to prompts. For this study, the investigators selected two Spanish and two Japanese courses that met twice per week for a total of three instructional hours. Each instructor conducted both traditional in-class OLA and digital voice-recorded OLA.

For the digital voice recordings, instructors, with the assistance of one of the researchers, assessed students' language proficiency using WebCT, a Web-based classroom technology system. Once logged in at the lab, students followed on-screen directions to record their responses in the second language (L2) to teacher-created prompts. The first prompt, randomly selected from 20 possible prompts, asked students to read a short, 40-word paragraph written in the L2 that contained descriptions of fictitious people. Students were allowed to take as much time as necessary to practice, record, listen to the recording, and rerecord the passage. Once satisfied with the recording, students saved the file with their name followed by a numerical one (1) to signify the first recording. Students then placed the file in the instructor's electronic folder for later retrieval and assessment.

Next, the computer displayed instructions for the second assessment to inform students that they had 60 seconds to answer an impromptu question. The students indicated their readiness to begin by clicking the "next" button, and one of 20 prompts was randomly assigned to each student on the computer screen. A digital timer counted down 60 seconds before the voice recorder automatically began to record student responses. Students were encouraged to maximize use of vocabulary, grammar, and L2 syntax as well as to speak for the entire time limit.

After one minute, the software instructed students to save the file with their names followed by a numerical two (2) to signify the second recording. Again, students placed the voice file in the instructors' folder before logging off the system.

For the in-class OLA, the instructors evaluated student proficiency during the designated weeks. The class day before the assessments, students were given examples of the two assessments and were told that the actual prompts would be slightly different. The day of the assessment, the instructors selected students' names from a box and assessed each individual student's oral language proficiency in a different classroom. Once students completed the assessments, they were excused from class and were requested to leave the building in order not to interact with students who had not yet been assessed.

Instruments

The researchers created an online survey using a 10-point Likert scale to ask students about their perceptions of traditional in-class OLA and digital voice recording assessments. Students were asked about their perceptions of anxiety, locus of control for success, accuracy of responses, amount of time they spent preparing for assessment, and vocabulary and structures usage in the L2. Instructors were interviewed about the two distinct procedures for OLA and were asked to discuss preference of OLA method, creation of artifacts to document student progress, issues of time management, administrative flexibility, and reliability of assessment.

Results

Findings from the survey and interviews with instructors and students indicate a perception that oral language proficiency was enhanced by using the traditional and technologically-enhanced methods of assessment. In an effort to avoid reporting complicated statistical findings, the investigators opted to report data using a more straightforward approach to demonstrate perceptions regarding the two approaches of OLA. To begin, survey data were retrieved from the database containing students' responses to the survey questions and were analyzed using a statistical software package.

The researchers first calculated Cronbach's Alpha, a measure of the degree of consistency for participants' responses on the survey, to determine the survey's reliability. A coefficient of .90 was determined, indicating that the participants' responses were very similar to one another. Next, the researchers analyzed means and standard deviations of individual survey items and then collapsed responses to form three groups for student responses: agreement, indecisiveness, and disagreement. Then, the investigators reported findings using percentages to indicate student perceptions of the two OLAs.

Table 1 shows a comparison of students' perceptions of traditional and digital voice recording methods for OLAs.

Table 1

Student Perceptions of Traditional and Digital Voice Recording for OLA

Traditional Method	Digital Voice Recording
-Students were more self-conscious and anxious. -Students reported higher levels of affective filter due to peer presence. -Students' answers in L2 were less authentic. -Students' responses were less creative.	-Students were more comfortable and relaxed. -Students' responses were more thorough. -Students noticed improvement in L2 learning ability. -Students spent time identifying their errors and improved oral language proficiency. -Students had a greater sense of control of their own success in L2. -Students experimented more with L2 vocabulary and grammar. -Students preferred recording answers for OLA. -Students were more willing to imitate native speakers.

For many students, the in-class OLA produced substantial self-reported anxiety. Of this group, 44% indicated feeling self-conscious when the OLA was conducted in class. Nearly a third of the participants (30%) felt they did not express themselves authentically in the L2, and even more (41%) felt their oral language performance was less creative. Additionally, almost half (44%) of the sample expressed a lack of satisfaction with the traditional procedure of in-class OLA when peers were present, because of a heightened sense of the affective filter.

However, 55% of the students using digital voice recording for OLA reported feeling more comfortable and relaxed recording their responses to OLA prompts in the language lab. Almost half the students (45%) reported preferring voice recording to traditional in-class OLA, while 15% of the participants favored the traditional method of oral assessment. Moreover, 44% also believed that their recorded responses were more thorough, and even more (55%) appreciated the ability to review, edit, and improve oral language proficiency using technology. Almost the same percentage (52%) reported that they were more likely to experiment with new L2 structures and vocabulary using digital recording technology, and 78% reported that they were more likely to try to imitate native speakers' speech when using voice recording. The majority of the students perceived that they had more control of their academic success (52%).

Interviews with course instructors confirmed student perceptions regarding the two approaches to OLA. Table 2 summarizes the main advantages of digital voice recordings.

Table 2

Instructors' Perceptions of Traditional and Digital Voice Recording for OLA

Traditional Method	Digital Voice Recording
-Is time consuming and disengages learners -Takes time away from instruction -Leaves more potential for classroom management problems -Is not replicable and does not allow for second opinion of student grade	-Increases instructional time in class -Allows evaluation to take place at unconventional times -Permits multiple opportunities for studnet success -Allows students to record responses at home or school -Leaves digital artifact for indication of student progress, accreditation data, and increased reliability of assessment -Encourages students to practice before turning to recordings

First, the instructors expressed concern about the traditional method of OLA, especially for loss of precious instructional time. The instructors reported that in-class OLA took approximately five to seven minutes per student, or the equivalent of almost two class periods. As the instructors assessed oral language proficiency with individual students in a separate room, problems of classroom management arose. Other instructors in the classroom area alerted the L2 instructors to disruptive academic behavior, such as loud discussions, students' showing videos on phones and laptop computers, and rearranging desks and tables. Instead of preparing for the assessments, many of the students (75%) self-reported engaging in social activities with classmates. Furthermore, student absence during OLA required instructors to extend office hours and give make-up exams.

Instructors said that in addition to increasing time for instructional and scholarly purposes, the digital voice recording offered flexibility in scheduling the time and place for the OLA evaluations. The instructors also reported having more freedom to grade student voice recordings in contexts that the traditional method could not accommodate, such as commutes to and from the university using iPods and MP3 players. On several occasions the instructors downloaded the files to home computers and evaluated student proficiency at times that best suited their busy schedules. Students also benefited from the use of technology. They felt a greater degree of control when using the voice recording strategy, and instructors noticed that most students recorded responses several times to improve the quality of their work. Students expressed themselves differently depending on the OLA procedure. Both instructors indicated that during in-class OLA, students were less likely to use newer vocabulary and grammatical structures and to completely answer teacher-created prompts. Students using voice recorders appeared to experiment more with the language and grammar, using a much broader vocabulary. Additionally, student response to questions was longer and many times more accurate using voice-recording software. Instructors commented that the rate of success of assignments increased when students were allowed to record their responses multiple times outside of class, rather than having only one opportunity to respond during in-class assessments. In fact, students said that they often practiced for hours before making a final recording to turn in for evaluation.

Instructors discussed other advantages of using digital artifacts over traditional oral assessment strategies. Over the course of the semester, several students had confronted the instructors regarding the accuracy of grading OLA using traditional methods, since student work could not be replicated in order to give a second opinion. Using archived voice recordings, other FL instructors were asked to listen to and evaluate student performance. The instructors agreed that digital files were more reliable than traditional methods and could be used to confirm assigned grades on OLAs. The recordings could also be used to document student learning progress over time, an important requirement for university accreditation.

Discussion

The authors see several implications of this study for FL educators. As school districts in many areas may face more stringent budgets, FL teachers can utilize a variety of free or affordable digital tools for oral assessment. The study indicates that using technology to assess oral skills appears to lower students' levels of self-consciousness and nervousness. Students reported feeling more creative when using technology than during traditional in-class assessments. Perhaps by utilizing available software, FL educators can encourage students to record responses for OLA in a non-threatening environment, building student confidence to use the L2.

The voice recordings also enhance accuracy and reliability in assessing student performances. Archived recordings can be replayed multiple times to calibrate scoring criteria and assure equity in grading by different instructors. Additionally, archived recordings can be used to demonstrate student proficiency during student conferences, and the files serve as a body of evidence to show progress toward meeting accreditation standards.

Instructors also reported that recordings saved valuable time and avoided many of the classroom management problems they normally experienced during in-class assessments. By using digital voice recording technology, FL educators can recapture more instructional time to spend with students. Additionally, digital voice recordings offer instructors more flexibility as to when and where they evaluate student performances. This flexibility might inspire FL teachers to assess student OLA more frequently, therefore helping to bolster student confidence and quality of performance.

The software can be downloaded for use both at home and at school. Students can use the described applications and devices with minimal training, and instructions for installation of software and the procedures for making recordings could be created and reused each semester. Parents or other students who see students using the devices might recognize the importance of technology and oral assessment within the FL curriculum. Clearly, as digital recording software continues to emerge, teachers and students alike can implement more technology to enhance FL instruction and learning.

References

Arturo, R., & Rupert, E. (2006). *Odeo* [software]. New York: Sonic Mountain. Audio file format. (2007, December 5). In *Wikipedia, The Free Encyclopedia.* Retrieved December 12, 2007, from http://en.wikipedia.org/w/index.php?title=Audio_file_format&oldid=175950196

Chan, M. (2003). Technology and the teaching of oral skills. *CATESOL Journal, 15*, 51-57.

Egan, K. (1999). Speaking: A critical skill and a challenge. *CALICO Journal, 16*, 277-293.

Egbert, J. (1999). Classroom practice: Practical assessments in the CALL classroom. In J. Egbert and E. Hanson-Smith (Eds.), *CALL environments: Research, practice, and critical issues* (pp. 257-271). Alexandria, VA: TESOL.

Flewelling, J. (2002). From language lab to multimedia lab: Oral language assessment in the new millennium. In C. M. Cherry (Ed.), *Dimension: Proceedings of the Southern Conference on Language Teaching* (pp. 33-42). Valdosta, GA: SCOLT Publications.

Fogg, B. J. (2005). *YackPack* [software]. Palo Alto, CA: Stanford University.

Foster, P., Tonkyn, A., & Wigglesworth, G. (2000). Measuring spoken language: A unit for all reasons. *Applied Linguistics, 21*, 354-375.

Mazzoni, D., & Dannenberg, R. (2000). *Audacity* [software]. Pittsburgh, PA: Carnegie Mellon University.

National Standards in Foreign Language Education Project. (1999). *Standards for foreign language learning in the 21st century.* Yonkers, NY: Author.

Volle, L. (2005). Analyzing oral skills in voice e-mail and online interviews. *Language Learning and Technology, 9*(3), 146-163. Retrieved December 8, 2007, from http://llt.msu.edu/vol9num3/volle/

5
The Teacher Work Sample in Foreign Language Education

Marat Sanatullov
Wichita State University

Abstract

Based on a sample WebQuest, the article analyzes how the Teacher Work Sample (TWS) and the preparation of foreign language practitioners can be implemented in light of contemporary theory, research, practices, and expectations for foreign language teaching, learning, and teacher education. The TWS framework emphasizes the integration of contextualized, proficiency-oriented, and assessment-driven communicative tasks, technology, and learners' multiple intelligences in the classroom.

Background

This article discusses how the Teacher Work Sample (TWS) can be used as a meaningful and relevant framework to scaffold pre-service foreign language teachers' preparation as well as integration and analysis of effective planning, instruction, assessment, and student learning in the foreign language classroom. The TWS is a major exit assessment that a teacher education program, an institution, and a state can require teacher candidates to complete in order to demonstrate effective teaching practices in relation to the subject area and grade levels of candidates' teaching certification. The author first describes the purpose, content, and structure of the TWS and reviews the vision and expectations for foreign language teacher education advanced by the *Program Standards for the Preparation of Foreign Language Teachers* (American Council on the Teaching of Foreign Languages [ACTFL], 2002). The purpose, content, structure, and expectations for field experiences in schools and a concurrent university methodology course designed for pre-service foreign language teachers are then presented in light of a required integration of a Practice Teacher Work Sample (PTWS). Finally, the author demonstrates and analyzes how different stages of the TWS can be effectively implemented in the preparation of foreign language (FL) teachers in order to have them focus on the understanding and integration of the profession's contemporary expectations for FL teaching, learning, and teacher education. Such expectations emphasize the use of contextualized, proficiency-oriented, and assessment-driven communicative tasks, technology, and learners' multiple intelligences in the FL classroom. The integration of the standards for foreign language learning, contemporary theory and research, and best practice is highlighted and illustrated by a sample WebQuest exploring French-speaking countries and cultures.

What is a Teacher Work Sample?

The TWS was developed by the Renaissance Partnership for Improving Teacher Quality, which represents 11 universities participating in this project (The Renaissance Partnership for Improving Teacher Quality, 2002). The TWS has seven interrelated sections labeled "processes . . . identified by research and best practice as fundamental to improving student learning," teacher planning, and teaching (Renaissance Partnership, p. 3): (1) contextual factors, (2) learning goals, (3) assessment plan, (4) design for instruction, (5) instructional-decision making, (6) analysis of student learning, and (7) reflection and self-evaluation. Each section or process is defined by its standard, the task that a teacher candidate has to accomplish, prompts to be followed, and a rubric that defines various levels of performance on the standard by teacher candidates. A TWS is based on an instructional unit that teacher candidates develop and implement in the classroom.

Teacher Education Standards

The *Program Standards for the Preparation of Foreign Language Teachers* (ACTFL, 2002) advances a comprehensive vision of what FL teachers are expected to know and do in order to teach the target language and culture effectively. While some standards underscore primarily the candidates' knowledge of the linguistic system of the target language, the target culture, and literatures, others assess the candidates' understanding and knowledge of the language acquisition processes, planning, instruction, and assessment in order to create a supportive classroom that reflects language outcomes and learner diversity.

Field Experience and Methodology Courses

At Wichita State University, teacher candidates are placed with a supervising FL teacher licensed or qualified to teach in their subject area and grade level to complete an 8-week placement at the 6-12 level (in middle or high school). During this field experience, teacher candidates develop, implement, and teach an instructional unit containing at least five lessons. Candidates develop and complete a PTWS based on the unit. Pedagogical content requirements for the unit reflect the profession's current expectations for FL teaching and learning as they are highlighted across the *Program Standards for Foreign Language Teachers* (ACTFL, 2002). Precisely, the PTWS unit should incorporate and demonstrate a contextualized approach to language teaching that emphasizes the use of meaningful language (e.g., Quests, stories, songs) with appropriate instructional strategies (e.g., reading strategies, TPR, storytelling, multiple intelligences), and technology (e.g., PowerPoint, video editing, Wiki) studied or discussed in the methods course.

To implement such requirements, teacher candidates are asked to use a WebQuest as the basis for their units. In the on-campus methods course, teacher candidates learn, discuss, and reflect on the purpose and structure of a WebQuest. First developed by Bernie Dodge in 1995, a WebQuest is a scaffolded learning structure that uses links to essential resources on the World Wide Web and an authentic task to motivate students' investigation of a central, open-ended question, development of individual expertise and participation in a final group process that attempts to transform newly acquired information into a more sophisticated understanding. (March, 2004, p. 1)

WebQuests "use constructivist approaches to learning, cooperative learning activities, and scaffolding within a socio-cultural learning environment" (Shrum & Glisan, 2005, p. 426). "The best WebQuests do this in a way that inspires students to see richer thematic relationships, facilitate a contribution to the real world of learning and reflect on their own metacognitive processes" (March, 2004, p.1). A WebQuest can contain six major interrelated Web pages presenting the following information: introduction (introduces the topic), task (defines the task), process (describes the steps of the inquiry), resources (contains the meaningfully organized Internet links), guidance (has organization and assessment tools), and conclusion (brings closure to the quest) (Dodge, 1997, p. 1).

In the on-campus methodology course, multiple teacher education strategies are used to scaffold novice teachers' unit development, such as microteaching, videotaping, providing feedback, and conducting writing workshops. During microteaching, teacher candidates select a lesson from their PTWS units and, during an on-campus class session, teach it to their classmates and university supervisor/methods professor to elicit their feedback. Pre-service teachers also videotape the teaching of an actual lesson from their PTWS unit taught in the school. Teacher candidates exchange the videotaped lessons and receive feedback from their peers, cooperating teachers, and university supervisor/methods professor and complete a self-evaluation of their teaching. Teacher candidates also participate in writing workshops, during which they discuss challenges, determine strategies for success, and exchange drafts and give feedback in relation to each section of their PTWS. Candidates revise, edit, implement feedback, and resubmit their PTWS drafts to the university supervisor/methods professor.

Such a teacher education process of the development and implementation of the PTWS engages and connects in various ways its four major participants—teacher candidate, language learner, cooperating teacher, and university supervisor/methods professor. The instructional areas of the interconnectedness between these participants are planning (using standards and language proficiency and developing objectives, lessons, and unit), assessment and instruction (developing and conducting pre-, post-, and formative assessments, measuring language learning), practice (conducting microteaching and writing workshops), implementation (teaching the unit in school and implementing modifications), and reflection and analysis (conducting discussions and brainstorming, videotaping and reflecting on taught lessons, analyzing data, and providing feedback). This process is based on weekly tasks included in the calendar of the placement; responsibilities of the teacher candidates, cooperating teachers and university supervisor during the field experience; and the schedule, content, and activities of the concurrent on-campus methodology course. Each week of the placement corresponds to the implementation of the new PTWS process, its supporting activities, and requirements.

Section I: Contextual Factors

For Section I, the teacher candidate "uses information about the learning-teaching context and student individual differences to set learning goals and plan instruction and assessment" (Renaissance Partnership, 2002, p. 5). This section includes school, classroom, and individual learner factors.

By using school and school district Web sites, teacher candidates gather and organize available information regarding school factors, specifically gender, ethnic, and sociocultural information about the school population. By using Microsoft's Excel program, students produce graphs that illustrate such school factors. For classroom factors, teacher candidates analyze the physical features, technology, resources and parental involvement, classroom rules and routines, grouping patterns, scheduling, and classroom arrangement in the classroom of their placement and teaching. Candidates create a map of their placement classroom containing the number and position of students' and the classroom teacher's desks, and the place and types of present technologies, blackboard, or whiteboard. In regard to student characteristics in the classroom, candidates are to address different student characteristics present in the classroom, such as gender, race/ethnicity, age, special needs, achievement/developmental levels, culture, language(s), interests, learning styles/modalities, and students' skill levels, including students' skills and prior learning that may influence the development of candidates' learning goals, instruction, and assessment. By using Microsoft's Word and Excel programs, candidates create charts and graphs that summarize student characteristics in the classroom.

Teacher candidates have to acknowledge that language learners can approach language learning in unique ways that reflect their multiple intelligences. Teachers' planning, instruction, and assessment should include appropriate venues to emphasize and develop the student diversity. As candidates develop this section of the project, they review in class that according to Gardner (1993, 1995, 1999), there are nine types of intelligences: intrapersonal/introspective, interpersonal/social, logical/mathematical, verbal/linguistic, bodily/kinesthetic, visual/spatial, musical/rhythmic, naturalist, and existential (identified and still being explored). Intelligence can be defined as "a biopsychological potential to process information" that can be activated "in certain ways" and in "an appropriate cultural setting" (Von Károlyi, Ramos-Ford, & Gardner, 2003, p. 101). There are five major language learning styles: analytical-global, intuitive/random, sensory/sequential learning, orientation to closure, and competition-cooperation (Oxford, 1990; Scarcella & Oxford, 1992).

Section II: Learning Goals

The standard in Section II of the TWS states that "the teacher candidate sets significant, challenging, varied, and appropriate learning goals." The section task for candidates is to "provide and justify the learning goals for the unit" (Renaissance Partnership, June 2002, p. 7). By using Bloom's Taxonomy of Cognitive Processes (Shrum & Glisan, 2005, pp. 455-456), proficiency guidelines, standards, and insights from theory and research, teacher candidates practice writing unit goals and lesson objectives, discuss and determine them with their cooperating teachers and supervisor/methods professor, show how they are aligned with local, state, and national standards, describe their types and levels, and discuss why they are appropriate in terms of development, prerequisite knowledge, skills, and other student needs.

Promoting Standards, Proficiency, Information Processing, and Cooperative Learning with WebQuests

Teacher candidates also review standards for foreign language learners and teachers (Communication, Cultures, Connections, Comparisons, and Communities), as well as proficiency guidelines developed by ACTFL in order to develop a rationale for integrating WebQuests in class (National Standards in Foreign Language Education Project [NSFLEP], 1999; ACTFL, 2002). For example, Cultures, Connections, and Comparisons are some of the content areas of language study addressed by WebQuests. Focusing on the relationships between the products, perspectives, and practices of the target culture, furthering students' "knowledge of other disciplines," acquiring information, and recognizing "the distinctive viewpoints," and comparing the target language and culture with students' own languages and cultures all serve to emphasize these content areas with WebQuests (NSFLEP, 1999, p. 9). Exchanging, interpreting, and presenting information according to the target proficiency levels (Novice, Intermediate, Advanced, and Superior) and sublevels (Low, Mid, and High) should be a communicative focus (NSFLEP).

Multiple levels and types of information processing leading to vocabulary and language learning that can be engaged with WebQuests are also discussed in the methodology course. In light of the constructivist approach to second language acquisition, WebQuest tasks engage learners' inductive reasoning when they formulate the general principles based on examples and details, enhance learners' metacognition (knowledge about the way one thinks) and awareness, contribute to both explicit and implicit language learning, and, consequently, heighten input processing and output production (Ellis, 2001). In the explicit language learning, students learn language with a conscious focus on grammatical, lexical, or syntactic language features of language, while in the implicit language learning, they do it without such awareness. If input processing concerns the way language learners internalize and understand language forms to which the teacher exposes them, output production is the students' use of the target language. Generative, communicative, and enhancement input and output tasks, negotiation of meaning, collaboration with others, problem-solving and elaboration, relation between vocabulary and the goal of activities, organization of information, use of inferring, cues, visuals, frequent exposure to input, extensive reading and writing, and learners' background knowledge lead to vocabulary and language learning (Brown, Sagers, & LaPorte, 1999; Coady, 1997; Hulstijn, 1992; Kost, Foss, & Lenzini, 1999; Newton, 1995; Paribakht & Wesche, 1997; Rott, 1999).

Teacher candidates also analyze several cooperative learning models focusing on problem-solving or exploration that are conceptually similar to the rationale and purpose of a WebQuest. Problem-solving models recognize the importance of finding solutions in learning and include several steps, some of which are identifying the problem, selecting and implementing an appropriate strategy, and evaluating solutions (Bruning, Schraw, & Ronning, 1999). On the other hand, exploration models enable the teacher to organize students into research groups to explore a particular topic of inquiry. For example, the Group Investigation Model has several steps that contain the teacher's presentation of an inquiry/topic: student group formation and task distribution; the identification, analysis and presentation of resources and data; and evaluation (Slavin, 1995). In the Original Jigsaw and Jigsaw II Models, students work in learning groups to study an academic topic or material (Slavin, 1995), and groups assign tasks to different group members to become experts about a particular aspect of the topic in order to inform their group members about the acquired information.

Sections III (Assessment Plan) and IV (Design for Instruction)

For the Task in Section III of the TWS, teacher candidates are asked to design "an assessment plan to monitor student progress toward learning goal(s)", and "use multiple assessment modes and approaches aligned with learning goals to assess student learning before, during, and after instruction" (Renaissance Partnership, 2002, p. 8). In Section IV, Design for Instruction, the teacher candidate "designs instruction for specific learning goals, student characteristics and needs, and learning contexts" (p. 11).

The use of a WebQuest illustrates how the measurement of student learning, especially during the instruction of a unit, can be implemented in an integrated, step-by-step, and contextualized manner. A model WebQuest has been specifically developed by the author and used for demonstration, reflection, and instructional development purposes with teacher candidates. It gives a rationale for and specific examples of formative assessments, activities, and materials that can guide teacher candidates in the development and implementation of their own units and related WebQuests. Teacher candidates also learn that Web development (e.g., Micromedia Dreamweaver), multimedia (e.g., PowerPoint, HyperStudio video editing software), or word-processing programs (e.g., Microsoft Word) can be used to build the pages and activities for a WebQuest in order to upload them to the Internet, project them on the classroom screen, or place them on lab computers to be used by students. As an alternative way of conducting such projects, the pages can be printed on hard copies and distributed to the students in class. To learn and practice how to use the relevant technologies, candidates participate in technology sessions of the methods course.

A Model WebQuest

"France, Maroc, Viêt-Nam, et Canada: A travers Continents, Histoire, Cultures, et Langues"
[France, Morocco, Vietnam, and Canada: Across Continents, History, Cultures, and Languages]

Pre-service teachers learn that this WebQuest is about the Festival of the World Cultures in New York, organized by the United Nations (UN) in order to affirm the uniqueness of different cultural and linguistic communities and to continue to battle against prejudice and racism in the world. The UN invites representatives and learners of different languages and cultures to give presentations on the communities that speak those languages. Following this invitation, Abdou Diouf, Secretary General of the International Organization of French-Speaking Communities, announces a competition to choose the presentations that will best represent the French-speaking world at the festival. The final part of the competition will take place on the island of Martinique in the French Antilles. According to the established criteria, presentations should be creative, reflect the multicultural and multiethnic diversity of the French-speaking world, represent countries from different geographical areas, and contain references and examples from different areas of knowledge and life. To do so, language learners are organized into teams of four to six participants for a competition to select the best presentation. By completing the WebQuest, every team prepares a creative presentation representing four French-speaking countries (e.g., France, Morocco, Vietnam, and Canada) across four content areas (e.g., geography, history, culture, and languages). At the end, all students vote to choose the best presentation.

Teacher candidates discuss the objective of this WebQuest, which is to foster the linguistic proficiency and sociocultural competence of language learners, as well as their cognitive and social development. It is designed primarily for novice and intermediate learners of French at grade levels 9-16. Teachers, however, can adjust, modify, or extend the discussed sample activities to tailor them to the developmental and language proficiency levels of their students as well as to the specific instructional goals and objectives. By engaging in discussion, brainstorming, and cooperative learning and by using scaffolding, facilitation, and the expertise of the university supervisor/methods professor, teacher candidates determine the tasks, functions, and text type that can be used with a WebQuest at each stage of the project. They may then synthesize their findings in a table and compare them with a model summary developed by the supervisor/methods professor.

At the Introduction page/stage, language learners are engaged in pre-reading tasks, such as recalling information, guessing, discussing, defining, comparing, and predicting. Reading strategies include scanning and skimming the text, locating information, identifying ideas, and answering questions. At the Task page/stage, students complete post-reading activities, such as reviewing the text and defining and discussing the task; and at the Process page/stage, students read/develop and implement the steps of the inquiry. They consult resources at the Resources page/stage; use guiding and assessment instruments at the Guidance page/stage; and reflect, analyze, and summarize at the Conclusion page/stage.

To complete this assignment, students complete the first two items on a KWL chart. They first fill in the "K" ("What do you Know?") and "W" ("What do you Want to know?") columns. The third column of the chart, "L" ("What have you Learned?") is completed at the end of the inquiry. Learners are exposed to different kinds of written text discourse, such as titles of the pages/stages; the "K" and "W" columns of the KWL chart and Venn diagrams at the Introduction page/stage; introductory text at the Introduction and Task pages/stages; steps of the inquiry at the Process page/stage; list of resources at the Resources page/stage; rubrics and charts at the Guidance page/stage; and column "L" on the KWL chart at the Conclusion page/stage. Candidates also determine the areas in which WebQuests engage and connect language learners and teachers. Pre-service teachers create an advanced graphic organizer reflecting the found ideas and compare them with the model provided by the university supervisor/methods professor. Such areas include language learner diversity (language proficiency, multiple learning styles, and intelligences), types of inquiry (problem solving and exploration Quests), other disciplines (technology, psychology, and applied linguistics), teacher competence (language proficiency, knowledge of standards, theory, research, instructional methods, target culture, and students' use of technology), and structure of the Quest (six interconnected pages/stages).

Teacher candidates complete the activities in the model WebQuest in order to explore, experience, reflect on, and discuss what the teacher and learners do while completing such a project. The WebQuest, its activities, and materials can be written and presented in the language that teacher candidates teach, in English, or in the original language of the project (e.g., French).

Introduction

During the introduction to the WebQuest, language learners visit the Introduction Page of the WebQuest, which contains the title of the project, the introductory text, and Web links to the other pages of the WebQuest.

Pre-Reading Activities

Before reading the introductory text, the teacher sets the stage for the inquiry by activating the learners' interests and establishing their knowledge in relation to the topic. Several pre-reading activities can be used to anticipate the investigation. The teacher announces to the class that students will complete a project called "WebQuest," explains to them what a WebQuest is, and asks whether students have previously participated in a similar project. Then the teacher asks students to read the title of the WebQuest in the target language and think individually, with a peer, or in a group, about what studnets might have learned or want to know about this topic. To complete this assignment, students fill out the "What do you Know?" (K) and "What do you Want to know?" (W) columns on the KWL chart. The third column of the chart , "What have you Learned?" (L), is completed at the end of the inquiry. Proficiency-based questions developed by the teacher guide the students' brainstorming in relation to the chart. To give answers, students can consult textbook materials, dictionaries, or notes. As a culminating activity, with a peer or in a group, students share and discuss their entries in the KWL chart and complete a Venn diagram for which they organize similarities and differences between the countries in question.

Introductory Text

The introductory text in the target language represents the general context of the inquiry. As necessary, the content, length, structure, vocabulary, and grammar of the text can be adjusted to students' developmental and language proficiency levels as well as to teachers' specific goals and objectives.

Reading Strategies

The purpose of the reading strategies should be the activation of learners' existing linguistic (vocabulary, grammar) and cultural knowledge, as well as the integration of new relevant material that prepares students for the content of the WebQuest. Learners can be asked to scan and skim the introductory text in order to complete individually, with a peer, or with a group, a text map in the form of a graphic organizer that asks learners to give information about the structure of the text. Learners locate information in the text and make entries on the map regarding the main and supporting ideas, setting, problem, and solution, as well as their own opinions with respect to the context of the text. By following a model of the map presented by the teacher and produced with the Inspiration software program, students can draw a map on a piece of paper on which they enter selected and summarized information. A handmade map serves as a reflection and brainstorming instrument for learners' interaction with the text.

Task

During this post-reading phase, the class visits the Task Page of the WebQuest. Students are asked to review in the introductory text the purpose of the Quest and share and discuss it with a partner or a group. In order to assist the students with their reading, the teacher may prepare in advance a brief summary of the task based on the introductory text. This technique, which requires students to read the summary and explain the task, is especially useful for those with lower levels of language proficiency.

Process

On the Process Page, the class goes over the process steps designed to explore the topic of the WebQuest. These steps should be specific and measurable and considered as learning strategies used to explore the topic. Particular grammatical points and vocabulary topics across proficiency levels can be addressed, such as the use of the imperative, present, and future tenses, vocabulary employed for suggestions and orders, sentence structure, and different levels of discourse. Some examples of this project follow:

Etape 1: "Les étudiants forment quatre groupes d'exploration afin de préparer une présentation." [Step 1: Students form four exploration groups in order to prepare a presentation.]
Etape 2: "Au sein de chaque groupe d'exploration, chaque étudiant choisit d'explorer un pays en particulier des quatre pays avec un groupe d'experts."
[Step 2: Within each exploration group, each student chooses a particular country to explore with an expert group.]
Etape 3: "Dans les groupes d'experts, les étudiants explorent les pays de leur expertise."
[Step 3: In the expert groups, students explore the country of their expertise.]
Etape 4: "Les étudiants retournent dans leurs groupes d'exploration pour partager ce qu'ils ont appris et continuent leurs recherches en préparant leurs présentations finales."
[Step 4: Students return to their exploration groups to share what they have learned and continue their search by preparing final presentations.]
Etape 5: "Chaque groupe d'exploration présente sa présentation à la classe que tous les étudiants évaluent."
[Step 5: Each exploration group gives its presentations to the class and all students evaluate them.]

Resources

Based on the countries and four content areas of the inquiry to be explored (geography, history, culture, and languages), resources are logically organized and located on the Resources Page. Searching and selecting Internet resources is a way for a teacher to build this page of the WebQuest.

Guidance

The Guidance Page can contain several tools, such as assessment rubrics for evaluating group presentations and individual members' participation and reflective (examples of maps and KWL charts) and guiding (content chart and list of tools for presentation) instruments used throughout the project (different steps) to represent multiple levels of feedback (self, peer, and teacher's assessment). Scoring levels can have word-based definitions, such as Outstanding, Good, Satisfactory, and Needs Improvement, with a corresponding number of points (e.g., Outstanding: 20 points). Content criteria of a rubric for presentations can be Quality, Quantity, Organization/Preparedness, and Creativity. Criteria for a rubric evaluating individual participation in groups can be Independence, Engagement, Cooperation, and Preparedness/Knowledge. The written definitions of the levels and criteria reflect proficiency and knowledge expectations and promote learners' reflectivity and collaboration.

Conclusion

On the Conclusion Page, in light of the completed activities, the teacher asks students to reflect upon what they have learned during the WebQuest. Students individually complete the column "What have you Learned?" (L) on the KWL chart and share their entries with their classmates. The teacher leads the class in summarizing students' outcomes on a KWL chart projected on a large classroom screen.

Sections V (Instructional Decision Making), VI (Analysis of Student Learning), and VII (Reflection and Self-Evaluation)

Finally, during and after the implementation of their units, candidates analyze and reflect on student learning and their own professional development. In Section V, Instructional Decision-Making, the teacher candidate "uses on-going analysis of student learning to make instructional decisions" and to report two examples of situations in which they have had to modify their original instructional design to reflect students' learning or responses (Renaissance Partnership, 2002, p. 12). For Section VI, Analysis of Student Learning, the teacher candidate "uses assessment data to profile student learning and communicate information about student progress and achievement" in relation to the performance of the whole class, subgroups, and selected individuals on learning goals. By completing the task in Section VII, Reflection and Self-Evaluation, the teacher candidate "reflects on his or her instruction and student learning in order to improve teaching practice" by analyzing both the learning goal where the students were most successful and the learning goal where students were least successful, as well as by reflecting on possibilities for professional development that the implementation of the unit and student learning suggest (pp. 14-16).

Conclusion

This article demonstrates how the framework of a Teacher Work Sample can be implemented during field experiences in schools and a concurrent university methodology course in order to equip FL teacher candidates with contemporary tools for planning, assessment, instruction, and analysis. The instructional model of the WebQuest is integrated into the development of a Practice Teacher Work Sample in order to guide novice teachers in creating and implementing the instruction and formative assessments for the units they are required to teach. A WebQuest developed for Novice and Intermediate learners of French, whose task is to explore a number of French-speaking countries in order to prepare presentations for the Festival of the World Cultures, is discussed as a model for a unit that reflects the profession's expectations for FL teaching, learning, teacher preparation, and development. WebQuests engage both Internet- and computer-mediated tools, as well as pedagogical resources that allow students to be primary players in the learning process. This activity both fosters learners' language proficiency and enhances their cognitive and social development. By incorporating authentic materials from the target culture and creating a meaningful context- and content-based learning environment, such relevant use of the Internet in a foreign language classroom supports and promotes students' socio-cultural competence.

References

American Council on the Teaching of Foreign Languages [ACTFL]. (2002, October). *Program standards for the preparation of foreign language teachers.* Retrieved on December 17, 2007, from http://www.actfl.org/files/public/ACTFLNCATEStandardsRevised713.pdf

Brown, C., Sagers, S., & LaPorte, C. (1999). Incidental vocabulary acquisition from oral and written dialogue journals. *Studies in Second Language Acquisition, 21,* 259-283.

Bruning, R. H., Schraw, G. J., & Ronning, R. R. (1999). *Cognitive psychology and instruction* (3rd ed.). Upper Saddle River, NJ: Prentice Hall.

Coady, J. (1997). L2 vocabulary acquisition through extensive reading. In J. Coady & T. Huckin (Eds.), *Second language vocabulary acquisition* (pp. 225-237). Cambridge, UK: Cambridge University Press.

Dodge, B. (1997). Some thoughts about WebQuests. Retrieved December 17, 2007, from http://webquest.sdsu.edu/about_webquests.html

Ellis, N. (2001). Memory for language. In M. H. Long & J. C. Richards (Series Eds.) & P. Robinson (Vol. Ed.), *The Cambridge applied linguistics series. Cognition and second language instruction* (pp. 33-69). Cambridge, UK: Cambridge University Press.

Gardner, H. (1993). *Frames of mind: The theory of multiple intelligences.* New York: Basic Books.

Gardner, H. (1995). Reflections on multiple intelligences: Myths and messages. *Phi Delta Kappan, 77,* 200-202, 206-209.

Gardner, H. (1999). *Intelligence reframed: Multiple intelligences for the 21st century.* New York: Basic Books.

Hulstijn, J. (1996). Incidental vocabulary learning by advanced foreign language students: The influence of marginal glosses, dictionary use, and reoccurrence of unknown words. *Modern Language Journal, 80,* 327-339.

Kost, K., Foss, P., & Lenzini, J., Jr. (1999). Textual and pictorial glosses: Effectiveness on incidental vocabulary growth when reading in a foreign language. *Foreign Language Annals, 32,* 89-113.

March, T. (2004). *What WebQuests are (Really).* Retrieved December 17, 2007, from http://www.ozline.com

National Standards in Foreign Language Education Project [NSFLEP]. (1999). *Standards for foreign language learning in the 21st century.* Yonkers, NY: Author..

Newton, J. (1995). Task-based interaction and incidental vocabulary learning: A case study. *Second Language Research, 11*, 159-177.

Oxford, R. L. (1990). *Language learning strategies: What every teacher should know.* Boston: Heinle & Heinle.

Paribakht, S., & Wesche, M. (1997). Vocabulary enhancement activities and reading for meaning in second language vocabulary acquisition. In J. Coady & T. Huckin (Eds.), *Second language vocabulary acquisition* (pp. 174-200). Cambridge, UK: Cambridge University Press.

Renaissance Partnership for Improving Teacher Quality (2002, June). *Teacher work sample: Performance prompt, teaching process standards, scoring rubrics.* Retrieved December 17, 2007, from http://fp.uni.edu/itq

Rott, S. (1999). The effect of exposure frequency on intermediate language learners' incidental vocabulary acquisition and retention through reading. *Studies in Second Language Acquisition, 21*, 589-619.

Scarcella, R. C., & Oxford, R. L. (1992). *The tapestry of language learning.* Boston: Heinle & Heinle.

Shrum, J. L., & Glisan, E. W. (2005). *Teacher's handbook: Contextualized language instruction* (3rd ed.). Boston: Heinle & Heinle.

Slavin, R. (1995). *Cooperative learning: Theory, research, and practice* (2nd ed.). Boston: Allyn & Bacon.

Von Károlyi, C., Ramos-Ford, V., & Gardner, H. (2003). Multiple intelligences: A perspective on giftedness. In N. Colangelo & G. A. Davis (Eds.), *Handbook on gifted education* (3rd ed.) (pp. 100-112). Boston: Allyn & Bacon.

6

Connecting a Standards-Based Curriculum with Student Performance and Assessment

Rosalie Cheatham
University of Arkansas at Little Rock

Abstract

This article presents an approach to revising foreign language course and program assessment so that expectations for student performance and achievement in a standards-based curriculum reflect real-world contexts in which students learn to perform communicative tasks likely to be encountered in the target culture. Recognizing that many students choose to learn only the material that will be tested, this approach provides rationale and techniques to link instruction, practice, and assessment so that students will be motivated to use appropriate language and relevant technology to communicate on a variety of topics applicable to the target culture. Developing assessments that reflect accurately students' ability to use the language they have been practicing reinforces student motivation to perform to the highest possible level. Following the model of the ACTFL Integrated Performance Assessment (IPA) by which students are assessed within a specific content area across the three modes of the Communication Standard, this article presents both discrete assessment strategies and implementation suggestions for adaptations of the holistic approach of the IPA.

Background

The 21st century is clearly an age of communication. Middle school and senior high students have their own cell phones, justified as a necessary means of keeping in touch with parents. The era of social networking, from *You Tube* to *My Space* to *Facebook* to podcasts and vodcasts, encourages today's students to communicate constantly with peers because they can easily keep in touch with their group of friends and acquaintances. During the same decade in which the access to technology has grown exponentially and its usefulness has permeated our culture, the second language (L2) teaching profession has developed and embraced several key documents, including the *Standards for Foreign Language Learning in the 21st Century* (National Standards in Foreign Language Education Project [NSFLEP], 1999, 2006), which defines course content standards for L2 students. In addition, the *ACTFL Performance Guidelines for K-12 Learners* (American Council on the Teaching of Foreign Languages [ACTFL], 1998) focus on outcomes anticipated for the Communication Standard, and the *ACTFL Integrated Performance Assessment* guidelines (Glisan, Adair-Hauck, Koda, Sandrock,

& Swender, 2003) suggest strategies for a cyclical approach to assessing student performance within a specific content area of the Communication Standard. All of these projects encourage L2 educators to focus instructional goals and assessment on the learner's ability to communicate using real-world language.

Much of what is assessed today in L2 classrooms is achievement oriented, is not learner centered, and bears resemblance only coincidentally to real-world language usage. Students are required to turn off their cell phones and to disconnect from the social networks when they are in class in favor of learning language that is scarcely more exciting than the memorized basic sentences of the Sputnik era, such as "Une femme a été mordue au cou par le chien de son voisin et elle est tombée raide morte" (A woman was bitten in the neck by the neighbor's dog and fell over stiff dead) (Modern Language Materials Development Center, 1962, p. 247). In short, students are expected to stop using the communication strategies most familiar to them in order to perform the required and often contrived communication activities in the textbook. It is not surprising then that students, whether in K-12 or post-secondary-level classes, are not always enthusiastic about their language-learning experiences. As many states embrace standards and performance assessment rubrics for K-12 programs in an effort to encourage real language performance, the dissonance with instruction in postsecondary environments grows, since senior university faculty often remain stubbornly isolated from the standards movement. At the university level, retention of students beyond the minimum number of courses required remains a challenge.

Students decide quickly what is really important in any course after the first test, when they see what and how content is tested. No matter what the teacher says is important, the test demonstrates to the student the content mastery that will be required to achieve the desired letter grade. All too often L2 students find that the practical activities prior to the exam are vastly different from the exercises on the unit test.

This article describes an articulated connection between instructional design, course content, and course and program assessment in a university French program that extends and adapts the K-12 models for the post-secondary, standards-based curriculum utilizing evolving technologies wherever appropriate. The benefit of organizing instruction and assessment around the three modes of the *Communication Standard*—Interpretive, Interpersonal and Presentational (Standard I), is that *Communicative Performance* is assessed consistently throughout the program. The intentionality of valuing *Cultural Perspectives* (Standard II) and *Comparisons* (Standard IV) and the opportunity to utilize content from a variety of sources championed by the *Connections* (Standard III) and *Communities* standards (Standard V) provide the opportunity to merge instructional goals with real-world learner outcomes.

Connecting Students with Course and Program Expectations

Whether they realize it or not, students enter classes with both positive and negative expectations. Many, if not most, elementary-level college students, have studied a second language at least briefly at some point earlier in their academic career. They enter L2 classes thinking they know what to expect, having chosen the class in which they enrolled because they have heard that the teacher is good, the time suited them and their current work schedule, they did not want the other teachers listed for the class, or a friend was already enrolled in this section. They expect the class to be either hard or easy and take the class because they have to complete a requirement, not necessarily because the course content will be of interest or matter in their lives. If they have had positive experiences before or have already achieved a level of mastery in another language, they bring expectations that the new language will be learned the same way the other language was. They believe they know how to study, and they have a strategy—good or bad—for the amount of time and types of assignments they will choose to complete.

Intermediate students have studied in high school or in a previous college semester, not necessarily recently, and have formed study habits that satisfied the expectations of their previous French instructors. They have retained some content knowledge from previous courses, but their proficiency is often in the novice range. The unevenness in proficiency evidenced by students enrolled in advanced skills courses is even more significant than that of intermediate students. Learning strategies for both groups are entrenched and perhaps fossilized. To make a significant impact on today's students, a broad-based change in instructional content and methodology is essential. A standards-based communicative approach offers one such solution.

Motivation Matters

Since students have performance expectations already formed, it becomes critical to engage them in a different set of outcome expectations from the start. The importance of wanting to succeed is clearly not limited to success in L2 classes. There is an almost axiomatic awareness in our culture that success comes to those who are motivated to work tirelessly toward a specified goal, that nothing worth doing comes without effort, and that wanting to win is more than half the game. Graham (2004) observed in a recent study that the concept students have of their abilities and motivation to learn a second language may be enhanced by improving the learning strategies they employ to access and retain the language they are studying. For all of the energy and research in L2 acquisition strategies in the last half century, workbook exercises in current textbooks have hardly enabled a new generation of language students to transfer the vocabulary from the exercises into facile communicative competence, in part because the assessment instruments remain largely objective, right or wrong, teacher- or publisher-driven, machine-graded, externally standardized, and rewarded even by our profession's own testing programs. The work on which the students perceive they are graded is still too often disconnected from real-world language usage.

An initiative to formulate an assessment designed to measure students' progress toward the national standards resulted in the development of the IPA. The developers of the IPA note that there have been many research studies related to the importance of connecting instruction and assessment, yet there remains a "widespread use of classroom achievement tests and standardized instruments that still rely on easily quantifiable testing procedures with frequent noncontextualized and discrete-point items" (Adair-Hauck, Glisan, Koda, Sandrock, & Swender, 2006). Further, "information gleaned from these tests does not inform the stakeholders as to whether or not our students will be able to perform authentic tasks in the real world" (p. 363). The authors further observe that the traditional paradigms of testing remain in part because

> teachers often find it a daunting task to switch from traditional testing formats, which offer more control for teachers, to more open-ended formats, which may pose challenges in terms of scoring for teachers who are not familiar with this type of assessment . . .[and that] . . . performance-based or authentic assessment requires too much class time. (Adair-Hauck et al., p. 363)

Demands for improved learner outcomes exist at the post-secondary level as well, but to date they have focused more on program productivity and assessment than on student assessment and performance. Still, the *9 Principles of Good Practice for Assessing Student Learning* approved by the American Association for Higher Education (1996), while focused on programs, imply that the importance of moving toward authentic assessment is perhaps even more important in the post-secondary environment, since the ability of the college graduate to use the knowledge gained to perform in the real world is an immediate goal following graduation.

The French faculty in the Department of International and Second Language Studies at the University of Arkansas at Little Rock reorganized the French curriculum in 2004 (Cheatham, 2006, p. 81) to reflect a standards-based approach in which all courses are revised and subsumed under a standard (e.g., Pronunciation under the Comparisons Standard, French Cinema under the Connections Standard). It is now incumbent on the faculty to ensure that unit, course, and program assessments focus on real-world applications of the language studied. This structure requires a well-articulated plan for performance assessment and standards mastery and is less centered on a lock-step progression through the curriculum. If, as Conrad (1999) observed almost a decade ago, "most students tend to cease formal foreign language study as soon as they have fulfilled the requirement whether or not they have cultivated a useful level of foreign language proficiency for themselves" (p. 494), then motivating students to embrace this real-world holistic view so that they leave the program with functional competency is a significant task. (See Appendix A for curriculum design.)

Technology and the Interpretive Mode

Whether students enter the program at the elementary, intermediate, or advanced level, the first classes are designed to inform new students or remind returning ones that the goal of the class is performance-oriented and that they bear significant responsibility for the success of the learning process. For example, from day one of a French I class, students are challenged to deal with real language of the day. Since classrooms are now equipped with the technology necessary to stream video from the Internet, a first-day listening activity is to watch and listen to a brief news clip from that day's *Télématin* broadcast available from *France 2*. Similar to listening to a broadcast of the *Today Show*, this activity serves several purposes. It immediately demonstrates to the students that the language is real and that news stories in France bear a striking resemblance to those in the United States since, more often than not, the top story of the day is the same as one that would be broadcast here. With the appropriate instructor guidance, students realize that they have in fact understood some of the story. The utilization of streaming video begins to strip away the perhaps subconscious belief of the students that they know what to expect from the class. Thus, their attention is captured differently than would be the case with a more traditional "opening act" for the class, such as utilizing the introductory video that accompanies the text or simply presenting the initial chapter greetings.

The video segment is followed by a print media article downloaded and copied from a French newspaper of the day, usually on a topic of international interest or one about a well-known personality. Following the video segment with a print-based activity enables students to feel comfortable immediately, as they realize that they can understand more of the written article than was possible with the televised piece. Using questions that encourage the student to make logical guesses, infer meaning, and connect the article to their own interests and knowledge, the instructor is able to guide the students toward a willingness to try new approaches to studying and learning. Assessment of interpretive learning begins as students are challenged, motivated, and rewarded with authentic materials. The advantages of this approach are validated by recent studies that reinforce the long-held belief that guiding students to comprehension and accuracy through inductive reasoning and contextualized input remains the most effective way to engage students actively in the learning process (Haight, Herron, & Cole, 2007).

One key purpose of the day-one activity is to challenge the students' attitudes toward what they think they are going to learn to do with the language and to help them recognize from the beginning that they have the skills that would enable them to survive if they were in the target culture instead of inside a classroom at an American university. Many are surprised that they are able to comprehend a significant portion of the content. Clearly, the gisting, skimming, and scanning strategies applied in this context are not new in L2 classrooms. However, the input is different. Using streaming video and audio in real time and newspaper articles downloaded daily via the Internet for instruction challenges the comfort level of some instructors, since it may not be feasible to spend the time in preparing to teach the content that would have been typical for the instructor in another setting. Maxim (2000) validates this assertion by documenting that the perceived inherent difficulty of authentic texts causes instructors to hesitate to include them as a central component of beginning language instruction. The teacher must be willing to let go of the need for thoroughly mastering content of material before allowing students to have access to it. This first step in letting go of control by the teacher continues when students are assigned to find an article from the Internet on a topic of interest to them. For purposes of this activity, they are encouraged to use <*leFigaro.fr*> in order to assure relative ease of access to a wide variety of potential topics.

Assessment includes common interpretive strategies, such as asking the student in English to indicate whether the article is primarily about a person, an event, or a location; when it took place; what meaning can be inferred by calling attention to cognates; and additional information students believe they understand. The ease of access to streaming video and free print sources from the Internet has increased dramatically in recent years, and students now have no difficulty accessing the recommended sites on their own. As a result, what started as a once-per-course activity has become a weekly expectation incorporated into the syllabus as part of the class participation grade. The assignments alternate between the students' selecting, printing, reading, and providing comprehension notes on an article from *Le Figaro* and listening to a 5-minute segment of *Télématin* from *France 2* and providing comprehension notes.

The value of connecting elementary course content to student interests is reinforced in a recent study (Hernández, 2006) that indicates that language acquisition and student persistence in continuing language study are positively influenced by "integrative motivation," the interest in interacting with native speakers of the target language culture. At the elementary level, this interaction begins with input from French media. It is broadened in subsequent courses, where students are expected to interact with native speakers, either in person or through the use of interactive technology. The critical change that influences interest, commitment, and performance is that students have significant control over the input. They choose topics that interest them and, as a result, they are more likely to work to understand what the article or broadcast is about. They become aware, subconsciously at least, that the language they are studying is useful and interesting, and they appear more willing to expend time and energy in preparing for performance-oriented assessments.

A common oral activity at the beginning of a class includes introductions and a demonstration of how to express simple likes and interests. Use of current technology can be of value in this context, as classroom introductions and information about personal interests may be easily modernized in an e-mail exchange between the students and the instructor. Students are asked to include appropriate salutations and reasonable information about where they are from, the courses they are studying, and their interests and hobbies. From this first e-mail exchange, class participation grades require additional e-mails to the teacher, e-mail exchanges among classmates on assigned topics, and the creation of class blogs to prompt interpersonal communicative practice. Students need to understand that these ongoing activities are key to mastery of course expectations or, as students may frame the issue, "What does it take to get a 'good' grade?" Assessment rubrics, explained more fully later in this article, are shared, so that students clearly understand from the beginning what they are expected to know and be able to do and, just as importantly at this beginning level, what they do not have to know. The first unit examination tests the students' skill acquisition in the same manner in which they have been learning and uses the same rubrics (Appendix B). The student receives an e-mail from the instructor and must respond appropriately. To assure fairness, a WebCT time-limited assignment window can be created, or the test can be administered in a controlled environment, such as a computer lab.

Even as assessments move into the realm of demonstrating performance capability, challenges remain for the instructor, since the text unit activities often do not match a functional context or content. Wiggins (1990) notes that the key difference between authentic and traditional assessment is that the authentic assessment requires students to be effective performers with the knowledge they have obtained. Traditional tests tend to demonstrate only whether the student can recognize, recall, or fill in what was learned out of context.

For example, most elementary textbooks include units focusing on the house and household furniture and related items. In some instances such vocabulary is related to a travel chapter and hotels. However, the vocabulary used in exercises for mastery and testing often consists of "bed," "dresser," "chair," "desk," "table," "painting," or "couch." Activities include describing a room or locating furniture using the correct prepositions. Although such activities serve to reinforce the core vocabulary, words such as "pillow," "pillowcase," "coat hanger," "hand towel," "light bulb," "outlet plug," and "current" that will far more likely be needed, are rarely included in an elementary course. If the assessment is to have a real focus, the more useful vocabulary is even more essential. The instructional modification is not to eliminate the core vocabulary but rather to expand it to reflect real situations where an extended vocabulary would be more readily needed, such as the following: "You've arrived at your hotel and your room doesn't have enough pillows. Talk to the clerk and request two extra ones, along with an additional bath towel." An elementary student can successfully negotiate this real-world interpersonal situation with practice and appropriate vocabulary and quickly recognizes the relevance of the course content. Additional authentic oral assessments include such activities as telling a cab driver how to find the house of your host family, asking the receptionist at the hotel for specific room requirements, explaining that something in the room does not work or is missing, and explaining to the attendant at an airline counter that you have left an important object on the plane on which you have just arrived. For oral practice and assessment, it is helpful to have a means of recording the exchange, so that assessment can occur after the exchange. Portable digital recorders provide an inexpensive technique for recording the performance. Their advantage over older technology is that the instructor can evaluate the production and easily share the evaluation with the student electronically.

In situations where a written document would be a normal means of communicating in the real world, the instructor develops an interpersonal or presentational activity and assessment. Writing e-mails to a friend to plan a weekend camping trip or composing a note to a host family telling of the student's arrival day and time are such examples. In these situations, accuracy of form and content are assessed. A similar focus on authentic performance continues throughout the elementary courses, although the activities and sources of authentic language vary. The unit on transportation and directions, for example, lends itself to interpretive assessment, as students learn to navigate the Paris subway. For assessment, the student must plan a day of sightseeing in Paris to locations from a list provided by the instructor. Having previously practiced using the subway, students prepare an itinerary for a well-organized day-long excursion to four sites around the city from a list of seven or eight possibilities provided by the instructor.

By the end of the course, students are accustomed to encountering authentic material, are sensitized to strategies that can facilitate their comprehension and survival, even in unknown situations, and have acquired significant sophistication in navigating and comprehending material from French Web sites. The summative course assessment is a project, not an examination, in which students prepare the materials necessary to participate in a summer study-abroad experience, including letters in electronic format to a potential host family, lists of items to pack, a plan for their first three days in Paris, a letter to fax requesting a hotel reservation, and a detailed excursion for one week to locations of their choice in France. Students include authentic transportation schedules and route maps and plans to "arrive" at the airport in Paris at least 3 hours before the scheduled flight departure announced by the instructor. In addition to the written elements of the presentation, students work in groups to present to the rest of the class some of what they experienced together on their week-long independent tour. This group interpersonal presentation includes at least one problem they encountered and how it was resolved. The other students must react by asking for more details and commenting about an interesting aspect of the presentation (Appendix B). As assessment follows instruction and practice throughout the course, students quickly learn that the productive expectations require that they learn not only the content but also the acquisition strategies that enable them to perform well on the unit assessment. It is this change that most clearly and distinctly encourages the elementary student to recognize the importance of performance.

The Intermediate Challenge

As students move from the elementary sequence, the content shifts to topics more commonly discussed among adults. This shift is an important component in recapturing in a new course the students' willingness to move beyond a level of comfort to a more sophisticated and proficient level. While students have reasonable confidence that they can make themselves understood on basic needs and are confident that they can infer essential meaning from authentic media sources, they have little capacity to converse or to respond to questions on topics beyond survival situations. If they are going to be motivated to persist, as Conrad suggests (p. 499), then opportunities to share ideas, attitudes, and opinions must be encouraged long before students attain the superior level of proficiency that is traditionally understood to be requisite to sustaining and supporting an opinion. Although students in elementary courses have demonstrated an ability to infer meaning from external sources, they lack the skills to connect the basic structural knowledge with the conceptual vocabulary they would like to use to share opinions in French. We enable students to discuss ideas and issues using the limited communicative strategies and structural accuracy they can reasonably demonstrate at the intermediate level, but the required skills must be taught and assessed.

This approach is beginning to be embraced by some textbook authors. The introductory material in one such text, *Controverses*, (Oukada, Bertrand, & Solberg, 2006) states,

> *Controverses*, as its title suggests, organizes a body of linguistic tic, cultural and academic knowledge designed for the French Intermediate level around social issues such as gender equity, globalization, immigration and bilingual issues. Using such competing topics as these, *Controverses* provides a content-rich intermediate program and promotes critical thinking through its underlying structure of *Point, Contre-point* and *Réplique et synthèse.* (p. IE-5)

This text provides content to serve as a bridge into the intermediate course objectives that require the learner to demonstrate the capacity to express ideas and opinions within selected contexts. Previously, the syllabus for the intermediate course followed a format similar to that of the elementary sequence but included more emphasis on oral and written comprehensibility and structural accuracy. With this new approach, students are guided to a much more sophisticated use of language, one that actually stimulates their interest in societal issues and increases cultural sensitivity and critical thinking. Attention to the Cultures, Comparisons, and Connections Standards is more substantive, since topics for discussion extend into these areas.

Students who began the study of French using the communicative approach described above find the transition to these intermediate course goals natural and reasonable. However, those who began their study of French using a traditional, non-communicative approach find this intermediate class challenging at first. The reason for the disparity between the two groups of students appears to be the level of comfort the communicative-approach students have obtained when approaching content that they do not completely understand. The reading and listening-for-the-gist activities that were used from the start in their elementary courses have become so routine that these students are willing, and in some cases eager to approach unfamiliar content in order to increase their communicative capacity. Those who are unfamiliar with the curriculum are much less confident that the course expectations are attainable. Therefore, in-class activities that mix students familiar with the program with those who are not are critical in order to convince the latter that the instructor is honest when insisting that it is not necessary to understand every word in order to communicate successfully and that assessments will, in fact, mirror input and practice activities. The students who appear the most challenged are those who have had very limited experience with authentic language prior to the course.

Whereas interpersonal activities were the most common and comfortable for students in the practice phase of the elementary course units, students at the intermediate level who are struggling to express ideas and opinions find that it is less stressful to prepare informational presentations. One requirement stated in the course syllabus is that each student utilize technology appropriately for at least two assessments during the course. For their presentations, some students chose to make PowerPoint presentations that incorporate sound files, while others created a blog and shared its contents. One student uploaded his material on a *Facebook* wall and invited other students to respond.

Since this approach has been used for only 2 years, it is too early to have statistical data to ascertain whether the performance of students as they complete their major is significantly improved by exposure to this content. However, it is clear from anecdotal feedback that students are more interested and willing to participate in these assessments than was true in a more traditional structure. It is reasonable to assume that if students are more interested and engaged in the preparation for their performance, whether in written or oral expression, it is likely that the level of proficiency will be at least as high as was previously true, and learner satisfaction will be higher. One reality is that the mastery of structure is less linear, since this holistic, communicative approach does not limit the verb tenses, pronouns, or adjectives students may use. For the instructor, the challenge is to set clear parameters that lead the students to focus on accuracy on the most important points for the particular activity. For example, in the unit about personal liberty and the common good, the structure content is usage of the future and conditional tenses. Therefore, setting up practice and assessment activities that ask students to discuss what they would do in a given situation or where they think society will be in coming to terms with the topic in 10 years helps the student gain some level of practical competency in using the unit structures. Since at this point the subjunctive has not been studied, the instructor assists students in structuring their communications so as to avoid the need for the subjunctive (a real-world communicative strategy) before the students try to use forms that are incorrect or become frustrated by wanting to use a structure that they have not yet studied. In almost every instance, these opportunities to learn circumlocution are valuable techniques for students whose greatest limitation is often their inability to find an alternate way to communicate the idea they wish to convey. These ongoing efforts to enable students to recognize that they often have enough capacity to express their ideas in French if they succeed in reframing their thoughts results in a greater communicative flexibility that is useful in more advanced courses.

The Advanced Approach

The remaining courses under the Communication heading (see Appendix A)—Interpretive Communication, Interpersonal Communication, Presentational Communication, and Conversation—are provided at the upper level and may be taken in any sequence. This change from the more traditional lock-step approach through the curriculum was created primarily to make it possible for students to enter courses leading to a French minor or major when the courses fit their schedules. Since not every course in the program is offered each semester, students can complete program requirements more quickly than if they have to follow a lock-step sequence. An unexpected benefit has been the fact that students learn that they can progress toward a goal from whatever point they enter rather than having to compare their competency to that of students with more experience. The use of formative assessments is of particular value because the instructor is able to provide feedback to individual students on their individual inaccuracies and offer activities that can help each of them progress toward enhanced performance.

Conversation courses have been a popular component of the curriculum for over two decades, and the revised structure gives them added prominence, since the required oral assessments lend themselves to real-world situations. Role plays and simulations are common activities, particularly where topics lend themselves to problem resolution. For example, a student studying abroad is housed with a family where one of the members smokes and the student is allergic to smoke. The activity requires that the student request a change of housing placement without offending the original host family. Another situation involves a problem with the heating unit in the student's apartment, requiring the student to provide detailed information about what caused the breakdown. An advantage to activities of this type is that students become familiar with the role-play component of an oral proficiency interview. Another common practice activity that works well for assessment is a debate format, in which students are divided into groups with an assigned side to promote a given topic. Topics used for these debates include such issues as control of advertising, "big-box-store" shopping as compared to online shopping or patronizing small merchants, and small-town living as compared to city life. The most popular among students is an activity in which small groups inform the other students as to how to do something. Although these activities begin as presentational communication, the assessment becomes interpersonal, as the audience asks for additional information or clarification of details from the presenters, who must then be able to explain the topic or concept well enough to satisfy the questioner. This activity encourages development of circumlocution skills for the presenters and also requires students in the audience to improve their questioning skills in order to seek the precise details they did not understand (Appendix B). A side benefit of these activities is that it encourages presenters to inform the class about a topic, event, or activity that interests them.

In the three-course series that focuses on cultural products, perspective, and practices, and perspectives of France and the Francophone world, the IPA is a useful tool for connecting the input phase of instruction with learning outcomes. In the course focusing on practices and perspectives of French culture, for example, units include such topics as traditional versus modern French family values; expectations of elementary, secondary and post-secondary education; and governmental, political, and judicial structures and how they impact French society and attitudes toward work and leisure time. Interpretive communication allows the students to access the information presented in the text and in other print media. It is clear from student performance and course evaluations that reading comprehension from authentic sources is significantly less challenging than was the case before the curricular revisions. Since the development of an understanding of the perspectives of the French is a core value of the course as reflected in the Cultures Standard, it is important to find ways to assess each student's acquisition of this understanding.

One interpersonal assessment requires a student to react to a situation as though he were French, while another student is expected to react as though he were American. The students are then asked to share their ideas and attitudes and to identify how their reactions were alike and different. Sample situations include assuming the role of a teacher (French or American) evaluating a student's essay and sharing the evaluation with the student, or of students (French or American) discussing what are the most important housing requirements for them (e.g., roommates, private room, bathrooms, dormitory amenities) while they are away at college. The presentational response may be oral or written. In either case, both communicative competence and cultural awareness are assessed. A variation on this technique is for the teacher to present a series of reactions or comments related to a particular topic and for the student to discern whether the statement was made by an American or Frenchman and to indicate on what basis the decision was made. A student, for example, having asked a teacher for help, then thanks the teacher for having taken time to provide assistance. Another situation involves what a participant says when young children misbehave in public. Most students can determine the appropriate source of the remark, but what they find difficult is the requirement that they articulate the basis on which the decision is made. This analysis leads them to a more highly refined and nuanced awareness of the perspectives that identify a culture.

For their final presentation, the summative assessment in the culture course, students are required to offer a research-based presentation in both oral and written form. Where possible, a component of the research involves an interpersonal exchange with a native of France. This exchange may be either in person or in electronic form, but the purpose is to further refine the student's ability to obtain and exchange information on a cultural topic of interest to the student. The result of this interpersonal component is then incorporated into the final presentation. This assessment, conforming to expectations within the Comparisons Standard, anticipates that the student will be able to demonstrate understanding of cultural distinctions and similarities between the French and Americans. A student interested in gymnastics, for example, interviews young French natives about their participation in organized sports and extra-curricular activities during an academic year and then presents the information gleaned and ties the interview results to the cultural concepts studied.

Under the Connections Standard, courses include a study of writings with an historical perspective, writings from a modern perspective, a course in French cinema, and various theme-based seminars. Interpretive communication skills for these senior-level students are so well ingrained that even though the content of the courses may be difficult, the students have acquired strategies and skills for approaching unfamiliar texts so well that they activate their own schema and read with both increased comprehension and increased satisfaction. Student responses show a clear improvement over their attitudes prior to the curricular revisions. Although the students' comprehension of films without subtitles remains challenging, their willingness to infer meaning based on the strategies for interpretive assessments learned in elementary courses seems to be encouraging a greater effort at comprehension. For example, when listening to unfamiliar material, students recognize that intonation patterns are helpful for finding key words and for inferring the attitude of the speaker. They have also acquired a capacity to re-engage in trying to understand, after having lost the stream of a conversation. The capstone of the program is a senior project that requires students to define a topic of interest to them and produce a summative research-based presentation, which is shared with faculty and other upper-level students. Topics presented recently have included a comparative analysis of the factors determining Oscar-winning and Prix César-winning films, an in-depth multimedia presentation on the daily life and cultural distinctiveness of Haiti, and a Web site for native French moving to the local area, a project that explained in detail all of the steps for French citizens to become acclimated to the local laws and practices, as well as connections required with French governmental agencies and policies for those living and working abroad. A fourth presentation was an adaptation of Rostand's *Cyrano de Bergerac* for presentation by the city's local children's theatre company. The quality of these presentations was a clear demonstration of the performance ability of the students, and the range of topics reflected the importance of allowing students to connect their studies with real-world interests.

Syllabi, Evaluative Guidelines, and Rubrics

As indicated earlier, the greatest research and emphasis on course-specific assessment has been at the K-12 level, where performance indicators and rubrics have been officially promulgated. For the university-level, standards-based assessments described above, performance indicators, rubrics, and an adaptation of the IPA are being used throughout the program. The syllabus for each course indicates that grading is determined largely (60%) through competency demonstrated in performance. Some traditional quizzes remain, but the percentage of the course grade assigned to such activities (20-25%) is minimized because it does not provide the kind of useful information to the learner or to the instructor that enables either to say with confidence that the learner has attained a requisite level of functional ability. In other words, it is difficult to test verb endings on a written quiz and ensure what the student is able to do with verbs in a real-life context. It is unlikely that any tourist walking down a boulevard in a foreign city has ever been stopped on the street and asked to complete a sentence with a correctly-spelled verb form, but acceptable performance requires that the verb be pronounced accurately. Written accuracy is required for the formative assessments (e.g., e-mails, *Facebook* postings and other real-world written communications) so that appropriate levels of accuracy can be required in the summative assessments. In the upper-level courses, a minimum passing score on the quizzes is established at 80%. From the standpoint of the instructor, a student who misses 20% of the material has not assimilated the structural knowledge adequately and will not perform well on the summative performance. From the standpoint of the student, a guarantee of a grade of 80% in this component of the course helps the student feel reassured about grading expectations.

In all courses at each level, outcomes and assessment are directly connected to in-class activities. In an attempt to reward appropriate effort rather than to penalize students for poor attendance, the grading includes a significant weight (20-25%) for class participation. If students are not in attendance, it is impossible for them to participate. Although this is a small detail, it connects to the overall strategy of training students that positive classroom behavior results in positive learner outcomes.

Following the guidelines developed for the K-12 performance indicators, the domains of the performance guidelines (i.e., comprehensibility, comprehension, language control, vocabulary use, communication strategies, and cultural awareness) are incorporated into evaluative rubrics. Guiding principles of the IPA have been embraced for establishing the rubrics. Individual performance is evaluated as to whether it exceeds, meets, or does not meet expectations. What meets expectations at the elementary level does not meet expectations at the intermediate level, and what meets expectations in advanced courses would exceed expectations at the intermediate level. In a few instances there are no descriptors for "exceeds expectations," since some materials do not lend themselves to that level of mastery. The weighted value of the particular domain varies according to the topic. In a particular 30-point activity, for example, comprehension, vocabulary use, and cultural awareness may each be evaluated with a 7-point range (21 total points possible), while the three remaining domains may be valued on only a 3-point range (9 total points possible). On another activity, each domain may have equal 5-point ranges.

An advantage of this system for students is that they understand that their grades are performance-based, rather than simply the result of a score on a traditional unit test. There is a clear connection between the strategies provided by the instructor during the interpretive phase, the activities in which the students communicate interpersonally, and the learning outcome demonstrated in presentations. This continuous cycling of content and productive strategies shows the students that they are progressing toward their long-range goal, and the program is resulting in better-motivated students. It is too soon to have enough empirical data to analyze whether this realization is the result of activities in which students were enabled to discern the gist from television broadcasts on day one of the elementary course; however, it is clear that the scoring rubrics coupled with the curriculum revisions have resulted in a more competent and satisfied student population.

Remaining Challenges

As refinement of the articulated content and assessment continues, the most significant challenge remaining is to define appropriate opportunities for utilizing technology to communicate. If language acquisition is to be authentic and useful in the real world, students should be able to keep their communication devices when they enter the language class. On the other hand, it is difficult to envision a time when text messaging in another language will be considered an acceptable demonstration of accurate language use. The present availability of online assistance and translation programs challenges the traditional expectations of having students produce their own work. L2 educators should develop teaching strategies that will integrate technology appropriately, utilize its benefits to engage student interest, and enhance student competency, if L2 education is to be relevant in the coming decades.

References

Adair-Hauck, B., Glisan, E. W., Koda, K., Sandrock, S. P., & Swender, E. (2006). The integrated performance assessment (IPA): Connecting assessment to instruction and learning. *Foreign Language Annals*, *39*, 359-382.

American Association for Higher Education (AAHE). (1996). *9 principles of good practice for assessing student learning.* Retrieved December 19, 2007, from http://ultibase.rmit.edu.au/Articles/june97/ameri1.htm

American Council on the Teaching of Foreign Languages [ACTFL]. (1998). *ACTFL performance guidelines for K-12 learners.* Yonkers, NY: Author.

Cheatham, R. (2006). Integrating standards and instruction: One university's experience. *Central States Conference Report,* 75-87.

Conrad, D. (1999). The student view on effective practices in the college elementary and intermediate foreign language classroom. *Foreign Language Annals, 32,* 494-512.

Glisan, E. W., Adair-Hauck, B., Koda, K., Sandrock, S. P., & Swender, E. (2003). *ACTFL integrated performance assessment.* Yonkers, NY: ACTFL.

Graham, S. (2004). Giving up on modern foreign language? Students' perceptions of learning French. *Modern Language Journal, 88,* 171-191.

Haight, C., Herron, C., & Cole, S. (2007). The effects of deductive and guided inductive instructional approaches on the learning of grammar in the elementary foreign language college classroom. *Foreign Language Annals, 40,* 288-310.

Hernández, T. (2006). Integrative motivation as a predictor of success in the intermediate foreign language classroom. *Foreign Language Annals*, *39*, 605-617.

Maxim, H. (2000). Integrating language learning and cultural inquiry in the beginning foreign language classroom. *ADFL Bulletin*, *32,* 12-17.

Modern Language Materials Development Center. (1962). *French, level two.* New York: Author.

National Standards in Foreign Language Education Project. (1999, 2006). *Standards for foreign language learning in the 21st century.* Yonkers, NY: Author.

Oukada, L., Bertrand, D., & Solberg, J. (2006). *Controverses.* Boston: Thomson Heinle.

Wiggins, G. (1990). The case for authentic assessment. *Practical Assessment, Research & Evaluation*, *2*. Retrieved December 19, 2007, from http://pareonline.net/getvn.asp?v=2&n=2

Appendix A

The standards-based organization for the major follows. It requires 30 credit hours above the elementary level, of which 9 hours must be senior-level courses. A grade of "C" or better is required in all courses.

- **Intermediate (3 hours)**

- **Communication (12-15 hours)**
  Integrated skills I – Interpretive Communication
  Integrated skills II – Interpersonal Communication
  Integrated skills III – Presentational Communication
  and Intermediate or Advanced Conversation

- **Cultures (3-9 hours)**
  Culture and Civilization I (practices / perspectives)
  Culture and Civilization II (products / perspectives)
  Francophone Culture

- **Comparisons and Communities (3-9 hours)**
  Pronunciation
  Advanced Listening and Pronunciation
  Practicum
  Senior project
  Study Abroad

- **Connections (3-9 hours)**
  Selected Readings
  Writings: Historical Perspective
  Writings: Modern Perspective
  Cinema
  Seminar (may be repeated for credit with topic change)

Appendix B

Interpretive Assessment – Elementary
Answers are to be completed in English.

	16-20	15 points	0-5
Interpretive (Comprehension)	Exceeds expectations	Meets expectations	Does not meet expectations
Understands main idea	Explains main idea in own words	Underlines key sentences referring to main idea	Is unable to find main idea
Comprehends key vocabulary	Infers meaning of more than 5 non-cognate key terms	Explains, from context, the general meaning of selected terms and cognates	Is able to define/translate fewer than 5 of the vocabulary words
Infers Author's attitude	Underlines words/phrases indicating author's attitude		
Infers cultural perspective	Identifies words/phrases related to cultural perspective		

Elementary Course Project – Group Discussions (2)

For this project, what meets expectations is specified as the standard. Points are added in areas where a student communicates significantly better than required, or points are significantly lessened when the student fails to communicate to the required standard.

	21 – 30	20 points each	10 – 15 each
	Exceeds expectations	Meets expectations	Does not meet expectations
Comprehensibility (4 points)		Participation in group discussions is comprehensible to teacher and most students.	
Comprehension (4 points)		Responds appropriately to cues and questions from group members, class members, and teacher	
Language Control (3 points)		Uses structures required to make the meaning understandable to teacher and most classmates	
Vocabulary Use (3 points)		Uses vocabulary required to complete the tasks and convey essentials of the group interactions	
Communication Strategies (4 points)		Is able to ask and answer questions adequately to survive the interaction	
Cultural Awareness (2 points)		Interactions are culturally appropriate	

Conversation Course

		25 points	
	Exceeds expectations	Meets expectations	Does not meet expectations
Comprehension (5 points)		Engages other students by asking and answering questions; demonstrates understanding of questions from teacher	Fails to understand questions from teacher and other students
Comprehensibility (5 points)		Generally understood by teacher and other students	Pronunciation problems impede understanding by teacher and other students
Language Control (5 points)		Conversation is generally accurate in present tense with limited control of past and future	Works mostly with memorized phrases, and tense inaccuracies mislead listeners
Vocabulary Use (5 points)		Uses vocabulary required to express ideas and appropriate to the situation	Works with mostly memorized cognate vocabulary
Communication Strategies (5 points)		Uses some circumlocution to answer questions for clarification	Is unable to explain or clarify ideas to listeners
Cultural Awareness		*Not assessed for this activity*	

7

The National Security Language Initiative and Less Commonly Taught Languages

Elvira Sanatullova-Allison
The State University of New York College at Potsdam

Abstract

In response to the events of September 11, 2001, and subsequent international developments, President George W. Bush introduced in 2006 the National Security Language Initiative (NSLI). The NSLI identifies a number of less commonly taught languages (LCTLs) as critical-need foreign languages and aims to further strengthen national security and prosperity in the 21st century by dramatically increasing the number of Americans studying these languages. To achieve this goal, under the direction of the President, various governmental agencies have developed a comprehensive national plan to expand U.S. foreign language education beginning in early childhood and continuing throughout formal schooling and into the workforce with new programs and resources. Since it may be too soon to note the effects of its implementation, NSLI's potential impact may be investigated by exploring the context surrounding this initiative, especially as it relates to LCTLs. This article examines the nature of LCTL learning and teaching, enrollment figures and trends, funding dilemmas, particularities of LCTL teacher preparation, and LCTL teacher equity and advocacy to shed some light on issues involving implementation of the NSLI.

Background

Paul Simon, the late senator from Illinois and a former chairman of the board of the National Foreign Language Center at the University of Maryland, noted in October 2001,

> In every national crisis from the Cold War through Vietnam, Desert Storm, Bosnia and Kosovo, our nation has lamented its foreign language shortfalls. But then the crisis "goes away," and we return to business as usual. One of the messages of Sept. 11 is that business as usual is no longer an acceptable option. (Simon, 2001)

Indeed, as we begin the 21st century, technological, economic, political, and social forces have created a new era. In response to the events of September 11, 2001, and subsequent international developments, on January 5, 2006, President George

W. Bush introduced the National Security Language Initiative (NSLI). The NSLI identifies less commonly taught languages (LCTLs), such as Arabic, Chinese, Russian, Hindi, Farsi, and others, as critical-need foreign languages. This initiative aims to further strengthen national security and prosperity in the 21st century by dramatically increasing the number of Americans studying these critical languages. To achieve this objective, under the direction of the President of the United States, the Secretaries of Education, State, and Defense, and the Director of National Intelligence have developed "a comprehensive national plan to expand U.S. foreign language education beginning in early childhood and continuing throughout formal schooling and into the workforce, with new programs and resources" (U.S. Department of State, 2006, p. 1). The President was to request $114 million in funding for the NSLI during fiscal year 2007. The initiative aimed at expanding the number of Americans mastering the critical-need languages has three broad goals: to encourage students to begin their study at a younger age, to increase the number of advanced-level speakers of foreign languages, with an emphasis on critical-need languages, and to increase the number of foreign language teachers and the resources for them (U.S. Department of State, 2006).

Because the NSLI was introduced less than a year and a half ago, it may be too soon to witness and assess the impact of its implementation, especially in the field of education. The first year of a new initiative is usually devoted to planning; so implementation would likely come at the end of 2008. Nevertheless, NSLI's potential impact may be investigated by exploring the context surrounding this initiative, with special attention to LCTLs, particularly those languages identified as critical-need foreign languages in the NSLI. An investigation of contextual factors related to the teaching and learning of LCTLs, enrollment figures, trends in both less and more commonly taught languages, funding dilemmas, particularities of LCTL teacher preparation, and LCTL teacher equity and advocacy may help shed some light on issues involving the implementation of NSLI. As Walker and McGinnis (1995) insightfully point out, "The study of less commonly taught languages . . . is not conducted in a vacuum. The study of all foreign languages and the broader educational concerns of our society must be considered when deliberating the directions of an educational field" (p. 1).

Less Commonly Taught Languages: An Overview

LCTLs, as Walton notes, "have their own world within American foreign language education: their own history, infrastructure, pedagogical traditions, financial support structures (however weak), and, of course, their own problems" (1992, p. 3). The National Council of Less Commonly Taught Languages (NCOLCTL, 2007) defines LCTLs as "all languages other than English and the commonly taught European languages of German, French and Spanish"; and the Less Commonly Taught Languages Project defines LCTLs as "all world languages except English, French, German, and Spanish" (Janus, 1998, p. 165). Other terms that are used to define this diverse group of world languages range from crucial, critical, strategic, neglected, rare, uncommon, less commonly spoken, and less commonly studied, to non-cognate, exceptional, and even exotic. The term LOTE (Languages Other Than English) is used in the state of New York, Australia, and the European counterpart of the National Council of Less Commonly Taught Languages, the European Bureau for Lesser-Used Languages (EBLUL). In the United States, however, most educators and authors prefer "the value-free and descriptive term 'less commonly taught languages' (or LCTLs)" (Janus, 2000, p. 1).

"A crude division" of LCTLs, according to Walton (1992, p. 1), recognizes three sub-groups: less commonly taught European languages (e.g., Russian, Italian, Portuguese, and Swedish), higher-enrollment non-Indo-European languages (e.g., Arabic, Chinese, and Japanese), and lower-enrollment non-Indo-European languages (e.g., Burmese, Indonesian, and Swahili). Walton goes one step further and, within the three groups mentioned above, identifies what he terms as "Truly Foreign Languages" (TFLs): the non-Indo-European languages as defined by the subgroups two and three, to distinguish them from languages that are cognate to English. Brecht and Walton (1994) subclassify LCTLs into four groups, according to the frequency with which they are offered at U.S. educational institutions: (1) the principal less commonly taught languages, such as Arabic, Chinese, Japanese, and Russian, that are generally available at U.S. colleges and universities, (2) the much less commonly taught languages, approximately 30 non-European, non-North American languages, such as Armenian, Czech, Hebrew, Indonesian, and Thai, among others, that have enrollments in the hundreds across the U.S., (3) the least commonly taught languages, approximately 80 languages that occupy a marginal position in the U.S. educational system and are offered at one or two institutions, and (4) the thousands of rarely- or never-taught languages.

When comparing the relative percentages of 17 different languages around the world with course enrollment at the university level, Janus (1998) notes that

> there is no overriding reason why U.S. foreign language enrollments need to mirror external factors such as total numbers of speakers in the world closely, but these comparisons show that languages with vast numbers of world speakers are neglected here as important languages to learn and speak. (p. 166)

Wiley (2004) believes that the United States has perhaps the world's most highly developed foreign language and area studies programs in the 131 National Resource Centers (NRC) and Foreign Language and Area Studies (FLAS) Centers and supporting 14 Language Resource Centers (p. 1). However, he laments the fact that the decision about which languages should be offered has been left to individual universities or individual faculty members. In order to assess the relative significance of languages for U.S. learners and to determine methods of delivery, Wiley proposes six guiding questions: (1) the number of speakers of the language; (2) whether the language is the primary language or a lingua franca for a nation; (3) whether the language is used widely in educational institutions, broadcasts, print media, and contemporary written and oral literatures; (4) whether the language is found in large amounts of archival materials for various disciplines; (5) whether the language is important because of its usage or significance politically, culturally, and socially; and (6) whether the language is important for U.S. national interests, such as scholarly research and use by business, media, foreign diplomacy and development assistance, and other government programs (p. 10). Taken together, these criteria would broaden cooperation within the language teaching community and inform decision making regarding the priorities of LCTLs (p. 10).

The National Council of Less Commonly Taught Languages is an umbrella organization for associations and individuals interested in less commonly taught languages. Inaugurated in 1990, the Council is currently headquartered at the University of Wisconsin-Madison. The goals of the Council are to find a way by which collective solutions to common problems can be developed and to provide a voice for organizations and individuals in the field of less commonly taught languages. The Council coordinates and conducts numerous projects and sponsors an annual conference on the less commonly taught languages. The Council is comprised of 18 different language associations with members in the United States and other parts of the world. These associations represent either individual languages, such as the American Association of Teachers of Arabic and the Modern Greek Language Teachers Association, or geographically defined language groups, such as the American Association of Teachers of Slavic and East European Languages and the South Asian Language Teachers Association. Each organization is represented in the Council by an official representative, and the officers of the Council are elected from and by the member organizations. The Council views its future as working toward securing a place for the LCTL agenda in a comprehensive national language policy, one that treats all American language needs as interrelated and vital to our future prosperity.

In July 2006, formal curricular and learning standards for Modern Standard Arabic were added to the *Standards for Foreign Language Learning in the 21st Century*, published by the American Council on the Teaching of Foreign Languages (ACTFL). First published in 1996, the current third edition includes guidelines for students at all levels studying 11 languages. The purpose of the standards is to establish common criteria with which educators can measure student progress at different stages of learning a language. These standards describe what students should know and be able to do across grade levels K-16, with specific sample progress indicators for grades 4, 8, 12, and 16. The standards for each language were developed and are revised by representatives of the organizations representing teachers of those languages, under the auspices of the National Standards for Foreign Language Education collaborative. Four LCTLs (Arabic, Chinese, Japanese, and Russian) now have standards, an invaluable accomplishment and an encouraging step toward the development of guidelines or frameworks for other LCTLs. In commenting on the NSLI, Dora Johnson, the Project Director of the K-12 Arabic Teachers Network of the Center for Applied Linguistics, points out that "there needs to be a plan put into place, [and this] plan must have the components of not only making programs available, but also the materials, the curriculum, the standards, and accreditation" (Zehr, 2006, p. 27).

Funding

Historically, support for the development and maintenance of LCTLs in higher education has been provided under Title VI, originally the 1958 National Defense Education Act and currently the 1965 Higher Education Act. These funds, however, have been used primarily for scholarly fellowships in area studies and not for material development, teacher training, curriculum design, or standardized test development (Walton, 1992). Although additional funding to enhance LCTL education has been provided by the U.S. Department of Education and private foundations, it has been viewed as inadequate by LCTL educators. To more fully fund the NSLI, the President was to request $114 million in the fiscal year 2007 budget proposal. One half of that total, $57 million, a $35 million increase over fiscal year 2006, was to be administered by the Department of Education and its partners to focus resources toward educating students, teachers, and government workers in critical-need foreign languages and to increase the number of advanced-level speakers in those languages. The sum of $24 million was to be used to create incentives to teach and study critical-need languages in K-12 by refocusing the Foreign Language Assistance Program (FLAP) grants. An additional $24 million would create partnership programs with school districts and colleges and universities to build continuous K-16 programs, with developing models for critical-need languages. Of the amount allocated, $5 million was designated to create a Language Teacher Corps, with the goal of having 1,000 new foreign language teachers, including those with proficiency in critical-need languages, in our schools before the end of the decade. An allocation of $1 million would create a nationwide Department of Education E-Learning Language Clearinghouse to deliver foreign language education resources, including those in critical-need languages, to teachers and students across the country. The remaining $3 million would expand Teacher-to-Teacher seminars to reach thousands of foreign language teachers. However, regardless of how promising and encouraging this increased funding may look, it presents some dilemmas. For instance, Scalera (2006), among other foreign language educators, notes that the NSLI educational funding "seems to bypass the most basic source of instruction in foreign language, that is, the K-12 institutions" (p. 11). Scalera also expresses a concern that the funding focused on critical-need LCTLs may divert desperately needed funds away from grants and scholarships for the approximately 90% of Most Commonly Taught Language (MCTL) learners in this country primarily studying French, German, Italian, and Spanish. Moreover, although the NSLI mentions the heritage community as a valuable contributor in meeting its goals and objectives, a closer look at the budget proposal reveals that it does not project any allocations to assist with the development or maintenance of programs specifically designed to help heritage speakers achieve the rigorous proficiency standards required for federal employment.

Learning LCTLs in the United States

"The United States needs to have a ready and steady supply of well-trained experts in many languages . . . and it takes a long time to develop expertise" (Janus, 1998, p. 168). Both the Foreign Service Institute (FSI) and the Defense Language Institute (DLI) have divided the various languages that they teach into four categories, based on the levels of difficulty for native English speakers to reach specified levels of proficiency. Approximate learning expectations for a number of languages taught at the FSI are based on the length of time it takes to achieve Speaking 3: General Professional Proficiency in Speaking (S3), and Reading 3: General Professional Proficiency in Reading (R3). According to the Interagency Language Roundtable (ILR) scale, proficiency level 3 roughly corresponds to the Superior Level of the ACTFL proficiency guidelines. The languages preceded by the asterisks (*) are typically somewhat more difficult for native English speakers to learn than other languages in the same category (Liskin-Gasparro, 1982; National Virtual Translation Center, 2007):

- Category I – Languages Closely Related To English (23-24 weeks, 575-600 class hours): e.g., Afrikaans, Danish, French, German (classified by the FSI as a category I language), Italian, Norwegian, Portuguese, Spanish
- Category II (30-36 weeks, 750-900 class hours): e.g., Bulgarian, German (classified by the DLI as a category II language), Indonesian, Malaysian, Swahili
- Category III – Languages With Significant Linguistic and/or Cultural Differences From English (44 weeks, 1100 class hours): e.g., Azerbaijani, Bengali, Czech, *Estonian, *Finnish, *Georgian, Hindi, Icelandic, Khmer, Lao, *Mongolian, Nepali, Pashto, Persian (Dari, Farsi, Tajik), Russian, Serbian, *Thai, Urdu, *Vietnamese, Zulu
- Category IV – Languages Which Are Exceptionally Difficult For Native English Speakers (88 weeks, 2200 class hours): e.g., Arabic, Cantonese, Mandarin, *Japanese, Korean

As we can see, the vast majority of LCTLs, particularly the ones identified as critical-need foreign languages, constitute the higher levels of difficulty in these groups, whereas MCTLs, namely Spanish, French, and German, are found in the ranks of the least difficult. According to Walton (1992), LCTLs are considered difficult and time-consuming for native English speakers to learn because of differences in the linguistic code (e.g., phonology, morphology, grammar, lexicon, orthography) or because of differences in the way that a language is used for interpersonal and interpretive intercultural communication, such as pragmatics. Walker and McGinnis (1995) point out that difficulties derive from writing systems that "differ from the alphabetic principle of the learners' base languages and from cultures that are not cognate with the Western tradition" (p. 5). Therefore, learners of LCTLs must spend more time than learners of MCTLs mastering skills.

However, if we estimate that the average college student receives 3 to 5 hours of instruction for 9 months, in addition to preparation time outside of class, we arrive at a figure of 108 to 180 hours of instruction per year. Given the figures above, it is not surprising that students who start learning a foreign language in college rarely achieve high levels of proficiency. This fact implies that the vast majority of institutions that provide opportunities to learn LCTLs cannot offer sufficient quantities of instruction for students to achieve an expert level of performance (Walker & McGinnis, 1995). "Although these practical considerations should not be stressed to the point that they discourage both teachers and learners, there is no way to avoid the matter of difficulty permanently" (Walker & McGinnis, p. 14). The inevitable conclusion is that in order to achieve high levels of proficiency as desired by the NSLI, the study of a LCTL should begin as early as possible and should be continued for many years, supplemented with summer classes and study abroad. Ray Clifford, former Chancellor of the Defense Language Institute, points out that "it's about time that U.S. educational systems provide the instructional time needed for language learners to acquire meaningful levels of language competence" (National Language Conference, 2005, p. 10).

Enrollment Patterns

Enrollment figures and trends at the K-16 levels reinforce the desperate need for early foreign language learning, especially in LCTLs. Foreign language enrollments in U.S. public secondary schools have increased slightly over the last few years, and, according to the last survey conducted by ACTFL, 33.8 % of students in grades 7-12 were enrolled in foreign language courses, as compared to 32.8% in 1994, the year of the previous survey (Draper & Hicks, 2002). Spanish continues to dominate, representing 68.7% of all foreign language enrollments in grades 7-12 in the United States, increasing almost 3% since the prior survey. However, in the other more commonly taught languages, the situation is not as encouraging. French enrollments were down 1.3%, and enrollment in German was down by slightly less than 1%, representing 18.3% and 4.8% of the total foreign language enrollments respectively in 2000. The only critical need LCTL included in the totals was Russian, which represented 0.2% of the 7-12 foreign language enrollment. Statistics for African languages, American Sign Language, Cantonese, Czech, Greek, Haitian Creole, Hebrew, Korean, Native American Languages, Polish, Portuguese, and Vietnamese were combined under a separate category. Chinese represented 1.44% and Arabic 0.62% of the 7-12 foreign language enrollment in this category.

It is important to note, however, that despite the call by the NSLI to begin foreign language education in early childhood and research in second language acquisition that overwhelmingly supports language learning at an early age, percentages in the earlier grade levels have dropped nationally, with only 5% of students in grades K-6 enrolled in foreign language courses in 2000 as compared to 6.4% in 1994 (Draper & Hicks, 2002). The distribution reflects the overall foreign language enrollment, with a strong lead by Spanish (62.4%), followed by French (19.6%) and German (1.2%), and with data available for only one critical-need LCTL, Russian (0.2%). Draper and Hicks conclude that "with the increasing dominance of Spanish, it will become incumbent on the foreign language profession to work with educators and policymakers to develop programs that will move students of Spanish into the study of other languages" (2002, p. 3).

The 2002 Modern Language Association survey of foreign language enrollments in U.S. institutions of higher education presents a similar distribution among MCTLs, with Spanish accounting for more than half (53.4%) of all enrollments, followed by French (14.5%) and German (6.5%) (Welles, 2004). Since 1968, French has lost 48% of its total enrollment and German 57.9%, a trend that continues to some extent into the present. While enrollments in Spanish grew 13.7% since the previous survey in 1998, French and German increased by less than 3%. These shifts in enrollment lead one to wonder if the numbers in French and German were lost primarily to Spanish, which "is becoming ever more significant in the undergraduate curriculum" (Welles, 2004, p. 24), or if the renewed interest in some LCTLs influenced students' decision as to which foreign language to study. Although LCTL enrollments still account for a small percentage of all foreign language students, the figures clearly show significant growth for some, if not most, critical-need languages. Enrollments in Arabic, for instance, increased 92.3% since the previous survey; Chinese grew at 20%, becoming the seventh more commonly taught language; Russian seems to have stabilized at 0.5%; Hindi showed remarkable growth at 72.1%; and Farsi went from 0 students enrolled in 1998 to 85 in 2002. There is also a considerable rise in the number of institutions offering Arabic and Chinese, while 29 institutions lost their German programs.

The table below shows the current records for various programs for the five critical-need languages, in the order listed in the NSLI, according to the Less Commonly Taught Languages Project database, sponsored by the Center for Advanced Research on Language Acquisition (CARLA, 2007), one of the U.S. Department of Education's Title VI National Language Resource Centers. This database also contains information on the number of locations in North America where students can study specific LCTLs.

Language	K-12	College	College (Summer Program)	Study Abroad Program	Distance Education
Arabic	67	333	27	57	7
Chinese	289	679	20	58	17
Russian	347	784	20	44	26
Hindi	1	110	6	12	1
Farsi	0	56	0	4	1

As the data show, at the K-16 level, Russian and Chinese are the definite leaders among the five languages, with Arabic and Hindi clearly gaining momentum. It is also encouraging to see growth in the study abroad programs in Hindi and Farsi.

What Influences the Study of LCTLs?

Walton (1992) argues that the typical student who takes a LCTL "may differ significantly in motivation and purpose" (p. 10) from the typical MCTL student. In a survey conducted by CARLA at the University of Minnesota (Janus, 1998), of about 60 LCTL teachers, more than half of them cited heritage as the primary reason their students enrolled. Other motivating factors included conducting research in social sciences or arts, studying international relations or business, relevancy for work or study abroad, personal or romantic relationships with native speakers of the languages, travel to the country, and attraction to the challenging and exotic nature of the languages. However, according to Walker and McGinnis (1995), "The overwhelming motivation for Americans to learn LCTLs is the intention to interact with the cultures of these languages" (p. 1). Walton found that "there is less concern with creating motivation than in maintaining and strengthening the learner's initial motivation as the complexity of the [LCTL] becomes apparent" (1992, p. 10).

LCTL Teaching and Teacher Education

"To the degree that [LCTLs] have unique linguistic and pragmatic features, it is only natural to expect different teaching practices" (Walton, 1992, p. 7) and a different approach to teacher education. However, the expansion of course offerings in LCTLs has not been matched by an accompanying acceleration in the amount or quality of LCTL teacher preparation, which is often identified as one of the most important needs felt by LCTL educators (Jacobson, 2001; Janus, 1998; Johnston & Janus, 2003; Schrier, 1994; Stenson, Janus, & Mulkern, 1998; Walker & McGinnis, 1995). Nina Garrett, Director of Language Study at Yale University, points out,

> We have nowhere near enough qualified teachers—and very limited prospects for training more than a handful of new ones—in the vast majority of the LCTLs which learners want and need to learn and in which the Nation needs proficiency. (National Language Conference, 2005, p. 10)

According to the *ACTFL Program Standards for the Preparation of Foreign Language Teachers* (ACTFL, 2002), teacher candidates should be able to communicate successfully in the three modes of communication—interpersonal, interpretive, and presentational—in the target language that they intend to teach. The expected level of proficiency for candidates is contingent on the specific target language as well as the native language, and these standards assume that the native language of the majority of candidates is English. As it takes longer for learners to attain high levels of proficiency in LCTLs, it consequently takes longer to reach levels of competency suitable to teach an LCTL than to teach an MCTL (Schrier, 1994). As mentioned earlier, the research conducted by the FSI shows that it takes more time for native speakers of English to develop a specific level of proficiency in certain target languages than in others. Therefore, for interpersonal speaking, candidates who teach French, German, Russian, and Spanish (groups I,

II, and III on the FSI scale), for example, must speak at a minimum level of Advanced-Low, and candidates who teach Arabic and Chinese (group IV on the FSI scale), for instance, must speak at a minimum level of Intermediate-High, as defined in the *ACTFL Proficiency Guidelines – Speaking* (ACTFL, 1999).

When it comes to the expectations for interpretive reading and interpersonal and presentational writing, candidates who teach target languages that use a Roman alphabet (e.g., French, German, Spanish) are able to attain a higher level of reading and writing skill in those languages because they do not have to focus on learning a new writing system. Candidates teaching languages that use a non-Roman alphabet (e.g., Arabic, Russian) or characters (e.g., Chinese) have to devote more time to learning the writing systems of those languages and may not initially reach the same level of reading and writing proficiency as their counterparts in target languages that use a Roman alphabet. In interpretive reading, for target languages that use a Roman alphabet, candidates will demonstrate understanding and interpretation at a higher level of detail than would be expected of those that work with target languages that use a non-Roman alphabet or characters. The same is true for writing. Candidates who teach target languages with a Roman alphabet must demonstrate a minimum writing proficiency level of Advanced-Low, while candidates who teach target languages that use a non-Roman alphabet or characters must demonstrate a minimum writing proficiency level of Intermediate-High, as described in the *ACTFL Proficiency Guidelines — Writing* (ACTFL, 2001).

Thus, expectations for pre-service teachers of LCTLs are different from those for their counterparts in French, German, and Spanish. Therefore, their preparation, although similar in many ways to that of MCTL teachers, requires differentiation, which must be understood by all members of the educational community, including administrators, supervisors, and even teacher educators, so that the development of the LCTL teachers can be effective (Schrier, 1994). According to the *ACTFL Program Standards for the Preparation of Foreign Language Teachers* (ACTFL, 2002), "the preparation of foreign language teachers is the joint responsibility of the faculty in foreign languages and education" (p. 2). However, since the majority of foreign language teacher educators are housed in MCTL departments, and consequently sometimes may not have a thorough understanding of the LCTL-specific acquisition and pedagogy, they tend to inappropriately generalize from an MCTL framework. Moreover, LCTL teachers' common personal characteristics are often not taken into consideration. For example, pre-service LCTL teachers are often older students, due in part to the fact that developing proficiency and content knowledge in these languages requires a greater length of time than in MCTLs. According to Schrier (1994), a conscious effort must be made to include within established foreign language teacher preparation programs elements that reflect the process of learning and teaching LCTLs in today's schools.

The LCTL Teacher Dilemma

Given the amount of time needed to achieve suitable proficiency to teach, many administrators hire native speakers of LCTLs as a quick fix for their staffing challenges. Walton (1992) observes that "the tradition of native target language teachers runs deep in the [LCTLs]" (p. 10), and the NSLI proposes to tap into the nation's heritage community to address and meet the need for advanced-level speakers in critical-need LCTLs. This call, however, regardless of how attractive it may be, must be approached with caution, especially when it comes to the K-12 educational context. For despite the overall growth in LCTL enrollments, examples of failed LCTL programs abound, and one characteristic that these programs have in common is that they were staffed by native speakers who had little or no professional educational preparation (Jorden & Lambert, 1991; Moore, Walton, & Lambert, 1992; Schrier, 1994). Administrators of these failed programs hired native speakers based on the assumption that the natural qualities these individuals possessed would be sufficient to successfully teach LCTLs.

Because native speakers can indeed have some valuable characteristics that are difficult to find in non-native foreign language teachers, such as linguistic and sociocultural competencies, they may add more authenticity to language instruction. "These desirable traits, however, do not always transfer automatically into good teaching" (Schrier, 1994, p. 56), especially if the native speakers are not properly prepared to teach native speakers of English. Jorden and Walton (1987) observe that LCTL native teachers do not always know what it is like to learn their native language as a foreign language or what it is like to function as a foreigner in their native culture. They may also lack the experience of having participated themselves as students within the U.S. educational system. Moreover, Walton (1992) notices that the view that native teachers have of their native language, their own experience in learning it, and their educational traditions may sometimes interfere with effective instruction of the language to foreign learners. In light of this dilemma, Jorden and Walton (1987) advocate an LCTL team-teaching model as an approach to ensure the best possible education in both language and culture for the U.S. student—a teacher from the learner's own culture working with a teacher from the target culture.

LCTL Teacher Equity and Advocacy

In her comments about the need for teacher equity and advocacy, Scalera (2006) notes, "If the situation is unstable for teachers of the [MCTLs], it is abysmal for those who teach [LCTLs]" (p. 12). Jacobson (2001), when discussing secondary foreign language teacher development, notes that "need for empowerment . . . is particularly desperate" for teachers of LCTLs (p. 2). While MCTL teachers, especially those in French and German, worry about losing their jobs, LCTL teachers "wonder when they will actually get paid a living wage for their skills" (Scalera, 2006, p. 12). Most LCTL instructors do not have full-time, tenure-track positions and resort to working as adjuncts, without benefits, to make ends meet. Low enrollment in some of the LCTLs often threatens the survival of entire programs and, therefore, the livelihood of those who teach these languages:

> People responsible for paying taxes that fund schools view this as a waste of money; the Russian teacher with 15 students being paid the same as a

Spanish teacher . . . with 30. Since the bureaucratic web reaches up from the tax payers to the school board, to the superintendent of schools, to the principal of the school, without support at any one of these levels, LCTL teachers find their programs and their positions threatened. Fighting for their program means fighting for their financial stability. This can be disempowering in that this "battle" goes on in isolation. (Jacobson, 2001, p. 19)

Indeed, if being an MCTL teacher can be a lonely occupation (Hammadou & Bernhardt, 1987), for an LCTL teacher sometimes it can mean total isolation. Schrier (1994) notes that "oftentimes, . . . LCTL teachers are '100% of the department' with no other colleagues who share their interest, enthusiasm, and expertise in their language" (p. 54). This separation from other disciplines is visited upon the LCTL teachers because they are in the unique situation of introducing a new language in an environment with previously established professional structures and performance expectations from the MCTLs.

Another particularly stressful and isolating professional situation facing LCTL teachers, but not part of the MCTL educational environment, is the dearth of adequate instructional materials, especially for K-12 classrooms. LCTL teachers and researchers are unanimous in their agreement about the scarcity, outdatedness, inappropriateness, high cost, and poor quality of teaching materials available for LCTL instruction, especially for the lower grade levels (Everson, 1993; Janus, 1998; Janus, 2000; Johnson, 1998; Johnston & Janus, 2003; Schrier, 1994; Wiley, 2004; Zehr, 2006). Although more materials have begun to appear, especially for Arabic, Chinese, and Japanese, Johnston & Janus (2003) "see grounds for cautious optimism as far as materials for at least certain [LCTLs] are concerned" (p. 7).

Additionally, meeting the in-service needs of LCTL teachers can be especially difficult. Many LCTL teachers can find professional development opportunities only during the summer, on their own time, and at their own expense (Jacobson, 2001). The challenge lies in the difficulty of reaching the teachers of these languages because of their small numbers. According to Schrier (1994), it is highly unusual to find more than five non-cognate language teachers within a 500-mile radius. Since it is impractical to create workshops for such a small population of teachers, the alternative is for LCTL teachers to go to conferences or summer language institutes for professional improvement. Indeed, the results of a recent LCTL teacher survey (Johnston & Janus, 2003) show that advocacy for LCTLs and for LCTL teachers, information about professional issues, and opportunities for collaboration were at the top of the professional development needs indicated by the teachers. The lack of government funding of professional development for LCTL teachers has always been one of the major equity and advocacy issues in foreign language education. "Without funding from external sources, LCTL teachers can neither keep up to date with new language-specific pedagogical information or find strength from interactions with colleagues" (Jacobson, 2001, p. 16).

LCTL teachers also "lack the numbers needed for their voices to be heard beyond their school systems [and] need to feel that they can do something about their situation" (Jacobson, 2001, p. 2). "It is only through increased public awareness . . . that LCTL teachers will be able to play a more central role . . . in the educational systems of which they form a part" (Johnston & Janus, 2003, p. 13). As Walton (1992) points out,

> To be a foreign language educator must surely mean to be concerned with the the teaching and learning of foreign languages beyond French, German, and Spanish. . . . Otherwise, we have the unfortunate division of "cognate language educators" versus "[LCTL] educators." There is a challenge here, one that involves the integrity of the field itself: that challenge is to become proactive rather than reactive in expanding the vision of foreign language education in the United States. (p. 14)

Conclusion

The issues surrounding the National Security Language Initiative are complex and multidimensional, particularly as they relate to less commonly taught languages. This article merely scratches the surface, and "more in-depth [empirical] research is needed" (Johnston & Janus, 2003, p. 14) to adequately assess and address the various related contextual factors, if the initiative is to produce expected outcomes. In addition to increased funding, action must be taken to address other needs, such as instructional time required for LCTL learners to acquire meaningful levels of language competence, specificities of LCTL teaching and teacher preparation, LCTL teacher equity and advocacy, and gaps in enrollment in LCTLs.

Although the NSLI specifically mentions Arabic, Chinese, Russian, Hindi, and Farsi, it adds "others" to the list of critical-need foreign languages. However, "critical language" is not a set list of languages, but rather an evolving concept (Scalera, 2006), and LCTLs of importance today may not be the same ones of importance in a decade (Walton, 1992). Thus, the concern is not so much for these specific LCTLs as it is for the state of foreign language education at large as an encompassing framework for educating "students who are linguistically and culturally equipped to communicate successfully in a pluralistic American society and abroad" (National Standards in Foreign Language Education Project, 1999, p. 7). As Scott emphatically points out,

> We have a critical national need to know other cultures and to be competent in communicating with other people. These are not new needs. We have heard many calls to action to address these needs. . . We have made so little progress and have prepared so many globally illiterate[citizens] because universities, states, businesses, and the federal government have been inconsistent in their priorities. . . . So it is past time for a renewed focus on our role as members of the world community. Last call; it is time for for action. (National Language Conference, 2005, p. 13).

References

American Council on the Teaching of Foreign Languages. (1999). *ACTFL revised proficiency guidelines – Speaking.* Yonkers, NY: Author.

American Council on the Teaching of Foreign Languages. (2001). *ACTFL revised proficiency guidelines – Writing.* (2001). Yonkers, NY: Author.

American Council on the Teaching of Foreign Languages. (2002). *ACTFL program standards for the preparation of foreign language teachers.* Yonkers, NY: Author.

Brecht, R. D., & Walton, A. R. (1994). *National strategic planning in the less commonly taught languages.* NFLC Occasional Papers. Washington, DC: National Foreign Language Center.

Center for Advanced Research on Language Acquisition [CARLA]. (2007). Retrieved December 10, 2007, from http://www.carla.umn.edu/index.html

Draper, J. B., & Hicks, J. H. (2002). *Foreign language enrollments in public secondary schools, Fall 2000.* Washington, DC: American Council on the Teaching of Foreign Languages.

Everson, M. E. (1993). Research in the less commonly taught languages. In A. O. Hadley (Ed.), *Research in language learning: Principles, processes, and prospects* (pp. 198-228). Lincolnwood, IL: National Textbook.

Hammadou, J. A., & Bernhardt, E. B. (1987). On being and becoming a foreign language teacher. *Theory into Practice, 26*, 301-306.

Jacobson, A. (2001). *Developing a voice: Teacher empowerment and second language teacher education.* (ERIC Document Reproduction Service No. ED 456105)

Janus, L. (1998). Less commonly taught languages of emerging importance: Major issues, cost problems, and their national implications. In J. Hawkins et al. (Eds.), *International education in the new global era: Proceedings of a National Policy Conference on Higher Education Act Title VI and Fulbright-Hays Programs* (pp. 165–171). Los Angeles, CA: University of California, ISOP.

Janus, L. (2000). An overview of less commonly taught languages in the United States. *NASSP Bulletin, 84*(612), 25-29.

Johnson, D. (1998). Less commonly taught languages. *The ERIC Review, 6,* 36-37.

Johnston, B., & Janus, L. (2003). *Teacher professional development for the less commonly taught languages.* Minneapolis, MN: University of Minnesota, Center for Advanced Research on Language Acquisition.

Jorden, E. H., & Lambert, R. D. (1991). *Japanese language instruction in the United States: Resources, practice, and investment strategy.* NFLC Occasional Papers. Washington, DC: National Foreign Language Center.

Jorden, E. H., & Walton, A. R. (1987). Truly foreign languages: Instructional challenges. *Annals of the American Academy of Social and Political Science, 490,* 110-124.

Liskin-Gasparro, J. E. (1982). *ETS oral proficiency testing manual.* Princeton, NJ: Educational Testing Service.

Moore, S. J., Walton, A. R., & Lambert, R. D. (1992). *Introducing Chinese into high school: The Dodge Initiative.* NFLC Occasional Papers. Washington, DC: National Foreign Language Center.

National Council of Less Commonly Taught Languages. (2007). Retrieved December 10, 2007, from http://www.councilnet.org/index.htm

National Language Conference. (2005). *A call to action for national foreign language capabilities.* Washington, DC: Author.

National Standards in Foreign Language Education Project. (1999). S*tandards for foreign language learning in the 21st century.* Yonkers, NY: Author.

National Standards in Foreign Language Education Project. (2006). S*tandards for foreign language learning in the 21st century* (3rd ed.)*.* Yonkers, NY: Author.

National Virtual Translation Center. (2007). Retrieved December 10, 2007, from http://www.nvtc.gov

Scalera, D. (2006). Should school districts redirect funds or resources toward developing new programs for critical languages? *New York State Association of Foreign Language Teachers Journal, 57*(3), 11-13.

Schrier, L. L. (1994). Preparing teachers of critical languages for the precollegiate environment. *Theory into Practice, 33,* 53-59.

Simon, P. (2001, October 23). Beef up the country's foreign language skills. *Washington Post.* Retrieved December 10, 2007, from http:// w.washingtonpost.com/ac2/wp-dyn?pagename=article&node=&contentId=A36489-2001Oct22

Stenson, N. J., Janus, L. E., & Mulkern, A. E. (1998). *Report of the Less Commonly Taught Languages Summit: September 20-21, 1996.* Minneapolis, MN: University of Minnesota, Center for Advanced Research on Language Acquisition.

U.S. Department of State. (2006). *National Security Language Initiative.* Washington, DC: Author.

Walker, G., & McGinnis, S. (1995). *Learning less commonly taught languages: An agreement on the bases for the training of teachers.* Columbus, OH: The Ohio State University Foreign Language Publications.

Walton, A. R. (1992). *Expanding the vision of foreign language education: Enter the less commonly taught languages.* NFLC Occasional Papers. Washington, DC: National Foreign Language Center.

Welles, E. B. (2004). Foreign language enrollments in the United States institutions of higher education, Fall 2002. *ADFL Bulletin, 35,* 7-26.

Wiley, D. (2004). *Collaborative planning for meeting national needs in the less commonly taught languages: Defining criteria for priorities in the languages of the world regions.* East Lansing, MI: Michigan State University, E-LCTL Project.

Zehr, M. A. (2006). Bigger education department role seen in Bush foreign language plan. *Education Week, 25,* 27.

8
The Belgian Connection

Lisa Signori
College of Charleston

Abstract

The land known today as Belgium is home to many important historical and cultural icons that many associate with France. Charlemagne, Jacques Brel, René Magritte, Georges Simenon, and even the ubiquitous "French" fries, all have an intimate Belgian connection. When one thinks of Francophone cultures, however, the focus normally turns to Africa, Québec, the Caribbean, perhaps Switzerland, but almost never to Belgium. This article presents a cultural unit on French-speaking Belgium that illuminates the country's linguistic and cultural geography, its history, politics, arts, and gastronomy. In addition to these basic culture capsules, the article offers suggestions for teaching and for pre- and post-assessment. This introduction to French-speaking Belgium is designed to encourage students to develop a broader cultural awareness of the diversity of the Francophone world and to appreciate its importance to them as world citizens. The impetus for this article comes from the author's experience in Mons in the summer of 2007.

Is Belgium Really a Country?

In 1953, the Belgian surrealist artist René Magritte wrote under his famous painted image of a pipe, "Ceci n'est pas une pipe" ['This is not a pipe']. More recently, a Belgian journalist put a different spin on that idea and gave the title "Ceci n'est pas un pays: Anatomie d'une nation imaginaire" ['This is Not a Country: Anatomy of an Imaginary Nation'] to the second chapter of his book, *Le complexe belge* (Crousse, 2007). Is Belgium really a country? Since the Revolution of 1830, when Belgium became an independent nation, many intellectuals have posed that question. Perhaps the best answer is provided in "Belgium: Society, Character and Culture. An Essay on the Belgian Identity" (Heylighen, 1998). The author writes,

> Although it is fashionable in some quarters to view Belgium as an "artificial state" put together by the European powers after Napoleon's defeat, history shows that the region which is now called Belgium has been almost continuously under a single rule since at least the 16th century. (¶ 5)

Yet there must be something in the cultural and political history of Belgium that gives rise to the question of the nation's "artificial" nature.

During the last 2,000 years, Belgium has been almost continuously occupied by outsiders— from the Romans to the Franks to the Spanish, and then the Austrians, the French, the Dutch, and, most recently, the Germans. The country has no major natural frontiers, such as mountain ranges or large rivers. Nor does it have a single national language, but rather three separate language communities. Flemish is spoken in the north, in Flanders; French is spoken in the south, in Wallonia; and German is spoken in a small corner of the east. This linguistic divide is emblematic of the way in which Belgium's powerful neighbors have influenced all aspects of Belgian history and culture.

The focus of this article is French-speaking Belgium, or Wallonia, the southern half of the country bordering France. Given Belgium's somewhat brief national history, its relative lack of strong national traditions, and Wallonia's small size and proximity to France, it should not be surprising that many aspects of Walloon culture have come to be associated with France, so much so that many of them are thought of as being French. Teachers recognize the uniqueness of the Francophone cultures of Africa, Québec, the Caribbean, and Switzerland. Belgium's Francophone heritage is just as unique. In fact, Clovis and Charlemagne, Georges Simenon, Inspector Maigret, French fries, and Trappist ales all have an intimate Belgian connection, and these are only the most well-known Belgian personalities and products. Educators have the responsibility to inform their students about Belgium's political and cultural geography, its history, politics, economy, arts, and gastronomy, thereby encouraging students to develop an understanding of Belgium's historical and cultural relevance in light of its position as the "crossroads of Europe" (Culture Briefing, 2007) in today's global world.

Culture Capsules

The study of culture is one of the Five Cs in the ACTFL *Standards for Foreign Language Learning in the 21st Century* (National Standards in Foreign Language Education Project, 1999). Language teachers today are expected to integrate cultural modules into the second language curriculum. Lange (1998), for example, recognizes this need when he states that "the growth of communicative approaches to the teaching of languages and the movement toward establishing content and performance standards for the learning of foreign languages have made the teaching of culture a requirement" (p. 25). Unfortunately, the cultural presentations in high school and even college introductory and intermediate-level textbooks are still often brief and sometimes superficial.

In this section, readers are offered a more detailed introduction to the culture of French-speaking Belgium. The goal is to enhance students' knowledge of the Francophone world by including a country that is overlooked when the other Francophone cultures are introduced. Before formally presenting the following information to students, teachers will find it useful to administer a pre-test to assess their knowledge of Francophone Belgium. An example of such a pre-test appears in Appendix A. In addition to the basic culture capsules, post-assessment and extension activities are provided. Several teaching suggestions are included, as well as ideas for two student projects that are both synthetic and communicative. Nevertheless, the author recognizes that teachers will have their own techniques and methodologies for the teaching of culture. The purpose of this article is to provide educators some basic information and resources to facilitate the integration of French-speaking Belgium into their cultural curriculum.

Geography

Belgium is a tiny country, slightly larger than the state of Maryland. It is bordered by the Netherlands to the north, Germany and Luxembourg to the east, and France to the south. To the west, the North Sea gives Belgium 66 kilometers of coastline. In the north, Flanders is flat, a point that Jacques Brel emphasizes in his song "Le plat pays"; out in the southeastern corner of Wallonia, the department of Ardennes is rather hilly. There are no mountains in Belgium other than, again according to Brel, belfry towers and church steeples. This geographical reality was surely appreciated by the competitors of the *Tour de France* who pedaled their way into Gand (Ghent) in the summer of 2007. Belgium's principal rivers are the Escaut, which provides the city of Anvers with its feeder to the North Sea, and the Meuse, which enters the country from northern France and continues to Namur, where it merges with the Sambre River. There are also numerous canals that meander through several cities, most notably the city of Bruges, aptly called the Venice of the North.

Belgium is divided into three political regions: Flanders, Wallonia, and the multicultural, multilingual capital of Brussels. The country includes 589 communes (towns and villages) comprising 10 provinces, each with its own main city, known in French as the *chef-lieu*. The five provinces in Wallonia are Hainaut (chef-lieu: Mons), Namur (Namur), Walloon Brabant (Wavre), Liège (Liège), and Luxembourg (Arlon). More information can be found on the "Géographie" section of the Portail fédéral de Belgique Web site at <www.belgium.be/eportal/index.jsp>. Interactive learning activities are available as well on the "Connais-tu la belgique?" Web page at <www.belgique.learningtogether.net/>.

Historical Highlights

The land known today as Belgium was dubbed by the Romans as Gallia Belgica when Julius Caesar conquered it between 57 and 50 BC (Cook, 2002, p. 2). The inhabitants living there were the Belgae, a Celtic tribe. Caesar (1952) recorded that of all the Gallic peoples, "Belgae sunt fortissimo omnium horum: propterea quod absunt longissime a culta atque humanitate Provinciae" ('The Belgae are the bravest of all these, because they are farthest from the cultivation and humanity of the provinces') (p. 2). Generally speaking, the Belgae ended up embracing Roman civilization and its contributions—stable government, technology, trade, and eventually Roman citizenship.

After the fall of Rome and the disintegration of its empire, the barbarian Franks crossed the rhine and settled in the area of Gallia Belgica. Their presence explains the origin of Belgium's linguistic divide. The northern region became German-speaking, while the southern half remained under Latin influence. By 431, the Franks had established the Merovingian dynasty and made their capital the present-day Walloon city of Tournai. Several Frankish kings who played significant roles in the development of France's history had Belgian origins.

Clovis I (465-511) was said to be born along the river Escaut. During his reign, he reunified under Merovingian control much of what had been Roman Gaul and moved the capital to Paris. In 496, Clovis was baptized and thus became the first Catholic Merovingian king, establishing a cooperative relationship between the crown and the Church that proved beneficial to both. After his death, the dynasty splintered, and there was never again a unified Merovingian kingdom.

Pepin the Short, born in Jupille in 714, deposed the last Merovingian king in 751, was elected king of the Franks, and established the Carolingian dynasty. Three years later, after Pepin gave him sanctuary, Pope Stephen II himself anointed and crowned him. This act converted kingship in Gaul into a divine right bestowed by God and also linked the Frankish throne with Rome in a near union of Church and state.

Charlemagne, the greatest of the Frankish kings, was the son of Pepin the Short, and grandson of Charles Martel. Born near Liège in 742, he inherited the entire Frankish throne in 771, ruling until his death in 814 in Aix-la-Chapelle (Aachen) (Cook, 2002). Charlemagne created a kingdom with a structure more advanced than that of his predecessors and was successful in preventing rebellions in his realm. He extended the limits of the Carolingian Empire until it reached from the English Channel to the Pyrenees, from central Italy to the Elbe River. On Christmas Day in 800, Pope Leo III anointed and crowned Charlemagne as the first Holy Roman Emperor. From the 9th to the 18th centuries, Belgian territory was controlled by the French, Dutch, Germans, Spanish, and Austrians. The Belgians ultimately could do little to affect the actions of their more powerful neighbors, but these circumstances began to change with the dawning of the 19th century. Huggett refers to Belgium as the "European Pawn," being the "area that remained after the great continental powers had temporarily wearied in the early nineteenth century of their struggle to carve out their own national territories on the face of Europe" (1969, p. 1).

In the wake of the French Revolution, "Belgium became an appendage of revolutionary France" (Cook, 2002, p. 49), when it was annexed by the new French Republic in 1794; and in 1804, Belgians officially became French citizens. Napoleon reigned over Belgium and was responsible for the creation of departments in Belgium. Church and state were separated, and the French Napoleonic Code was imported to form the basis for a new legal system. Under Napoleon's reforms, Belgium evolved into an industrialized state. Coal production increased, and metal and textile industries burgeoned. Although French dominance lasted only 20 years, it was influential because Napoleon imposed French as the official language in Wallonia. When Napoleon was defeated at Waterloo near Brussels in 1815, Belgium reverted under the rule of the Dutch House of Orange.

France's July Revolution of 1830 sparked a kindred revolutionary flame in Belgium, as many Belgians were predisposed to rise up against the Dutch. On

August 25, 1830, a performance of *La Mouette de Portici* at La Monnaie Opera House in Brussels touched off the Belgian "War of Independence." According to Adam (2007), who believes that his country is in many ways characterized by the absurd, one of the motifs of Auber's opera, *La Muette de Portici*, "Amour sacré de la Patrie" ('Sacred Love of One's Homeland') struck the revolutionary chord. When this aria was sung to the tune of "La Marseillaise," the bourgeois Belgians in attendance commenced their protest by ripping out the opera house seats (Cook, 2002, p. 57). Adam (2007) declared in a recent lecture, "A ma connaissance, c'est la seule [révolution] qui fût déclenchée par un air d'opéra" ('To my knowledge, it is the only [revolution] that was set off by an aria'). The rebellion spread immediately to the streets, where the bourgeois audience joined workers who were protesting against their Dutch bosses. Together they stormed the *Palais de Justice* and even took up "arms," throwing the contents of chamber pots on Dutch soldiers. This tactic worked, and by the next morning the Dutch soldiers had fled. By October 4, 1830, a provisional government declared independence, and 4 months later Belgium was recognized as a sovereign state by the major European powers. In 1831, the National Congress voted Leopold of Saxe-Coburg Gotha, uncle of the British Queen Victoria, King of the Belgians, and on July 21 he agreed to accept the office. Today, the 21st of July remains the country's national holiday.

The nation's first constitution was written in French, the only official language at the time, and this choice of language proved to be a point of contention for speakers of Flemish in the northern part of the country. Only at the end of the 19th century was Flemish recognized as Belgium's second official language. So, after a rather surreal revolution, Belgium, the nation, came into existence. The Belgian government today is a constitutional monarchy. Albert II is currently king, although the National Congress headed by the Prime Minister actually governs the country.

In what might be considered another surreal episode, Belgium joined the European colonial powers when it colonized the Congo in the 1880s. Before then, King Leopold I had refused to embark on colonial adventures. His son, King Leopold II, held no such reservations, and tiny Belgium gained political and economic control over a country 80 times its size. The Congolese consistently resisted Belgian rule, and this resistance led to repression that at times reached brutal degrees. According to Adam (2007), the Congo became Belgium's bargaining chip after World War II, when the Allied powers considered dissolving Belgian independence. In exchange for its continued sovereignty, Belgium agreed to supply uranium mined in the Congo for the development of the atom bomb. Thus Belgium survived intact in the aftermath of World War II. Demands for Congolese independence increased throughout the 1950s. In the wake of the 1958 First African People's Conference, Belgium finally agreed to withdraw its troops, and the Congo was granted independence on June 30, 1960.

Today, Belgium has become the political and economic crossroads of Europe. It was instrumental in the founding of both the North Atlantic Treaty Organization (NATO) and the European Union (EU). The capital, Brussels, has played a central role in recent European politics, becoming the seat of the European Commission in

1958 and of NATO in 1967. In addition, the central command of NATO military forces, SHAPE, (Supreme Headquarters Allied Powers Europe), is located roughly an hour south of Brussels, just north of Mons.

A wealth of information on Belgian history from pre-Roman to contemporary times may be found online. Three possible resources are "L'État belge: Petite histoire de la Belgique et ses conséquences linguistiques" at <www.tlfq.ulaval.ca/AXL/Europe/belgiqueetat_histoire.htm>, "Histoire de la Belgique" at <www.linternaute.com/histoire/histoire-de-la-belgique/ belgique.shtml>, and "Histoire" on the Portail fédéral de Belgique Web site at <www.belgium.be/eportal/index.jsp>.

Belgicisms

When French natives hear a French-speaking Belgian conversing, they often exclaim: "My, what good French you speak!" They seem amazed that people can speak "proper" French in Belgium, but it is the same language. In fact, Maurice Grévisse, one of the most famous French grammarians is Belgian; and Marguerite Yourcenar, Belgium's most famous female author, was the first female elected to the French Academy in 1980. There are, however, a few phonological and lexical differences between the French spoken in Belgium and that heard in France. Up to the beginning of the 20th century, residents of Wallonia spoke Walloon, a regional Romance language in its own right that is sometimes erroneously considered a French dialect, and many inhabitants spoke both French and Walloon. Walloon thus influenced the divergence of the French spoken in Belgium from that of France. Another factor contributing to the linguistic differences between the two was that Belgium has been politically separate from France for several centuries, except during the 20-year period of Napoleonic rule. The term "belgicism" refers to a word, expression, or turn of phrase characteristic of Belgian speakers of French. In fact, there are a number of online and hard-copy dictionaries that list many of these expressions (Lebouc, 2006; Massion, 1987; Tutoweb.com <www.tutoweb.com>).

Some belgicisms cause confusion because the same word has different meanings in the two countries. In France, breakfast is *le petit déjeuner*, lunch is *le déjeuner*, and dinner is *le dîner*. In Belgium, however, breakfast is *le déjeuner*, lunch is *le dîner*, and dinner is *le souper*. One day in Mons, the author was invited by a friend to *le dîner* and planned to join her at about 7:00 p.m. It was only when the host said over the noon break, "On va dîner maintenant?" that the author realized that the friend had been using the belgicism and had actually invited her to lunch. A *torchon* is a dish towel in France, whereas in Belgium, a *torchon* is a floor cloth; in France, a floor cloth is called a *serpillière*. To say "see you later," the French say "à bientôt" while Walloons say "à tantôt." A *mitraillette* in France is a machine gun, but in Belgium it is a meat-and-French-fry sandwich accompanied by the sauce of one's choice. Similarly, a *pistolet* in France is a pistol, whereas in Belgium, it is a roll generally eaten at breakfast. A *vidange* is an oil change in France, but in French-speaking Belgium it is the deposit paid on recyclable glass bottles. Other belgicisms can cause confusion because they are not used at all in current-day France. In Wallonia, *septante* is "seventy," and *nonante* is "ninety," as opposed to *soixante-dix*, and *quatre-vingt-dix* in France. Although *octante* ("eighty") may not appear in a dictionary of belgicisms, the author heard it used to the exclusion of *quatre-vingts* in French-speaking Belgium. Many weather-related terms are unique as well. Given the amount of rain that falls in Belgium, it is not surprising that the Belgians have a panoply of expressions to describe the many kinds of precipitation. A *drache*, for example, refers to a strong, steady rainfall. See Appendix B for more examples of belgicisms

Gastronomy

Belgium is home to a dense concentration of taverns and restaurants, and with good reason. Belgian cuisine is one of the most varied in all of Europe, enjoying Dutch, German, and French influences, as well as its own distinctive traditions. A few of the better-known Belgian specialties include *carbonnade*, a beef stew cooked in Belgian beer; *waterzoii*, a hearty cream-based soup made from a chicken or fish base; *speculoos*, molded cookies flavored with cinnamon and other spices; and endives, which were accidentally discovered by a Belgian farmer in 1830. Belgian endives are now consumed around the world. Nevertheless, when one mentions Belgian food, the imagination of most individuals will immediately turn to French fries, waffles, beer, and, of course, chocolate.

Belgian historian Gerard believes that *pommes frites,* French fries, were invented in the Meuse region of Belgium around 1680. He explains that the poorer inhabitants of this region often ate tiny fried fish; but when the river froze in the winter, they replaced the fish with potatoes cut to the same small size as the fish (<www.belgianfries.com>). But then why are they called "French" fries when the Belgians claim to have invented them? This question merits some reflection, and several interesting and plausible explanations for the misnomer exist. One is that when American soldiers stationed in Belgium during World War I first tasted them, they called them French fries simply because the locals spoke French. A second explanation has to do with the method of cutting the potatoes into lengthwise pieces, for in traditional English culinary terms, "to French" means "to cut into sticks" (as is the case with French-cut green beans); thus, the name French fries refers to the potatoes' being "frenched" (Original Belgian Fries Web site <www.belgianfries.com>). Of course, it could also be that fries actually were invented in Paris in the middle of the 19th century, as the French claim, even though no one can provide the name of the inventor. The Web site of Le Guide des connaisseurs at <www.leguidedesconnaisseurs.be/ article662.html> offers further discussion concerning the polemical origin of French fries.

In any case, the secret to Belgian fries is that the potatoes are twice fried. First, the potatoes are soaked in cold water, and then they are fried in oil at a lower temperature and allowed to cool before being fried again at a higher temperature. French fry enthusiasts believe that this double-fry method leaves the inside moist and the outside crisp and golden brown. Belgian fries are a popular snack on their own, sometimes sold at special outdoor stands called *frites* (*frietkots* in Flemish), where they are served in paper cones with a selection from a myriad of dipping sauces (mayonnaise is a favorite); or, if one prefers *au naturel* with just Some salt. When fries are accompanied by mussels cooked in white wine, they are called *moules et frites*, the national dish of Belgium.

Along with *pommes frites*, Belgian waffles are a popular snack, not as a breakfast or brunch item, as is the case in the United States. There are two main types of waffles in Belgium, those from Brussels and those from Liège. Brussels waffles are more like those we know as Belgian waffles in the United States. Of a uniform rectangular shape, they are often served with fresh fruit and whipped cream, although they may just be sprinkled with powdered sugar or coated with melted chocolate. Liège waffles, invented by a cook from Liège in the 18th century, are smaller, denser, irregularly shaped, and sweeter. Coarse sugar crystals are added to the batter just before it is poured onto the hot waffle iron and the sugar caramelizes on the outside of the waffle.

What would Belgium be without chocolate? Individual chocolates there are known as *pralines,* and the outer shell, sometimes sculpted into the shape of a seashell, is filled with a variety of fillings—cream, ganache, nuts, or liqueurs. The finer chocolatiers make their pralines by hand. Over 172,000 tons of chocolate are produced each year in Belgium and sold in over 2,130 chocolate shops. The road to good chocolate is not limited by region, for Flanders, Brussels, and Wallonia each has its own preferred *chocolatiers*.

More than for chocolate, Belgium is known for its beer, and more than 100 breweries produce between 400 and 800 varieties. In some restaurants the beer list is the size of a book. Moreover, when ordered in a café, bar, or restaurant, each beer is served in its own special glass, one specially designed to enhance that beer's particular flavor and aroma.

Of the many beers brewed in Belgium, the stars are the dark Trappist beers, the light *bières blanches*, and the sharply acidic lambics. Trappist monks originally moved to Belgium from France during the early 1800s, but they have been brewing since the Middle Ages. Their rich, dark beers are high in alcoholic content, from 6% to 12%. *Bière blanche*, on the other hand, is a lighter beer made from wheat. Numerous golden ales and abbey beers of varying degrees of body, flavor, and strength fill the spectrum in between. Lambic, the champagne of the beer world, relies on spontaneous fermentation; and, after up to 3 years of aging, it is corked like wine and sealed with a metal cap like beer. Some lambics have cherries or raspberries added, giving them an intense fruit flavor. More detailed information on Belgian beer may be found in *Michael Jackson's Great Beers of Belgium* (Jackson, 2007), as well as on the bierebel.com Web site at <www.bierebel.com>.

Fine Arts

For such a small country, Belgium has contributed significantly to the world of fine and popular arts. Out of French-speaking Belgium have come the saxophone, Art Nouveau, René Magritte, Jacques Brel, the brothers Dardenne, Tintin,

Lucky Luke, Inspector Maigret, and Hercule Poirot, to name a few (see Appendix C for other famous Belgians).

Art Nouveau was born in Brussels in the late 19th century. Victor Horta was a leader in this new architectural movement that eschewed straight lines, preferring feminine curves and floral designs, a reaction against the classical style that had dominated until then. Horta introduced this new architectural style in Brussels in 1893 with the construction of the Hôtel Tassel.

René Magritte is the most famous Belgian painter of the surrealist movement. His signature paintings include some of the most recognized and yet most enigmatic images of the 20th century: shoes becoming feet (*Le Modèle rouge*), a locomotive emerging from a fireplace (*La Durée poignardée*), a man without a face (*Le fils de l'homme*), and, of course, the pipe that is not a pipe (*La Trahison des images*). Magritte and his wife Georgette also lived in Paris for 3 years, where they met and became friends with surrealist poets André Breton and Paul Eluard.

Jacques Brel is perhaps one of the most famous French-speaking singers. Born in Brussels, though of Flemish descent, he gained fame living and working in Paris, and most of his songs were sung in French. His work also shows that he never forgot his origins. More recently, the brothers Luc and Jean-Pierre Dardenne have been making a name for themselves in the international cinematic world since their film *Rosetta* won praise at the Cannes Film Festival in 1999; they won again at Cannes with the film *L'Enfant* in 2005.

Other noted Belgians not always associated with their home country are actors Audrey Hepburn and Jean Claude Van Damme, both natives of Brussels, and structural anthropologist Claude Lévi-Strauss, whose work had a great influence on Roland Barthes, Michel Foucault, Jacques Derrida, and Jacques Lacan.

Popular Arts

The cartoon character Tintin is famous to French and English speakers worldwide. Tintin is the creation of Belgian Georges Rémi, whose pen name is Hergé. He introduced this comic strip in 1929 and followed its debut with more than 20 books. According to Tisseron (2002), Hergé "faithfully reproduced the xenophobic mood of his time, especially in *Tintin au Congo*" (p. 145). *Les Aventures de Tintin et Milou* reflected "the crises Europe experienced after 1930, particularly those having to do with racism and anti-Semitism" (p. 145). In spite of recent criticisms over how the Tintin series deals with racial issues, it is still Belgium's top international bestseller.

The comic strip occupies a somewhat exalted place in Belgian culture. Some of the other well-known French-language comic strips include *Lucky Luke* by Maurice De Bevère, the Smurfs (*Les Schtroumpf*) by Pierre Culliford, *Les Cités Obscures* by artist François Schulten and author Benoit Peeters, and the ever-popular *Le Chat* by Philippe Geluck. The latter two series are geared towards the adult reader. (Refer to Appendix D for a list of more comic strips popular with children and with adults.) Although Georges Simenon (1903-1989), Belgium's most prolific author, is best known for his pulp fiction, he was also well regarded in a number of literary circles. Born in Liège, he wrote more than 300 novels, 76 of which featured his most famous character, detective Inspector Maigret. Equally famous is Hercule Poirot, the Belgian detective created by Agatha Christie.

Pedagogy

How instructors present this material will depend on which aspects of Belgian culture they choose to include or have time to teach. This article does not offer suggestions for presenting Belgian literature or cinema, as teachers will have their own methods for integrating them into extant courses. But no matter what one decides to teach, it is recommended that a pre-test be administered to find out how much of the material the students may already know. Ideally, this activity will whet their appetites for more. Once the pre-test has been scored, the instructor can review in class the correct answers students were able to give; however, the incorrect answers should not yet be corrected by the instructor, nor should new material be presented. Rather, as a homework assignment, students can be required to revise their incorrect answers. This assignment provides an opportunity for investigative reports to be presented to the rest of the class, a communicative exercise in which the students become the teacher.

Once the instructor has determined which culture capsules to incorporate into the lesson plan, a range of pedagogical techniques present themselves. For example, basic historical and geographical information can be presented in lecture format or in more communicative activities, such as question-and-answer practice or oral summaries of readings (Lange, 1998, p. 14). Students can create crossword puzzles that review geographical, historical, and political information, as well as belgicisms and names of notable Belgians. When the crossword puzzles have been completed, they can be photocopied for the entire class. Comic strips offer a number of opportunities for communicative learning as well. Students can choose their favorite Belgian comic strip, delete the captions, and then make up their own captions, including as many belgicisms as possible. Students with an artistic bent can draw their own comic strips along the lines of models provided by the instructor. A variation on this idea is to have students complete the story line for a comic strip from which several frames have been deleted. One particularly effective exercise is to have students create a dialogue between a French speaker from France and one from Belgium and include belgicisms that can cause confusion between the two speakers.

After some background information on Belgian cuisine is introduced to students, the live demonstrations can begin. Students can find authentic recipes for Belgian fries and waffles (Brussels and Liège style) on the Gourmet Corner of the Belgium Tourist Office Web site (<www.visitbelgium.com>). They can, in groups, be responsible for supplying the appropriate ingredients; and with the necessary waffle maker or deep fryer, they can prepare waffles and *frites* in class. If cooking at school is not an option, then a chocolate tasting could be one of the highlights for this unit.

One effective synthetic communicative activity is a short research project. Students adopt the role of a travel agent, choose a principal city in one of the five provinces in Wallonia, and prepare a poster session or PowerPoint presentation about a day-trip from Brussels to the city. This report would include pertinent information, such as the city's history, industry, climate, population, location, local festivals, local food specialties, and points of interest. Useful resources for this project include the Belgian Railroad Web site at <www.b-rail.be/main/F/>, the *Le Petit Futé Wallonie 2008* (Dubrulle, 2007) guidebook, and its companion Web site, <www.petitfute.be>. An outline of this cultural project appears in Appendix E.

As a culminating communicative learning activity, a creative performance can tie together all aspects of contemporary culture. With careful guidance, students can prepare a newscast that includes food, "on-site" reporting from towns and villages to cover local festivals, weather, sports, literary interviews, and flash news bulletins. Before working on creating the newscast, the class as a whole can watch at least one Belgian television newscast via the Internet. For this purpose, the Web site for the Radio Télévision Belge de la Communauté Française (<www.la1.be/index.htm>) is especially useful. The entire class can decide how to divide up the news broadcast. One student, for example, may be designated as the news anchor to oversee and be responsible for creating the transitions between the news segments. The other students can work in groups of two or three, with a specific area assigned to each group. These students are the reporters, special correspondents, and the people who are to be interviewed. Following practice and rehearsal, the newscast can be recorded and subsequently used for recruiting and assessment.

At the conclusion of the cultural unit on Belgium, for the purpose of assessment, a post-test with the same questions provided in the original pre-test should be administered. Students should show a quantum leap in their knowledge about Belgium, as demonstrated by their ability not only to answer the questions, but to answer them confidently and in detail.

Conclusion

Belgium surprises with its many contributions to Francophone culture. What is often assumed to be French may not be. The information and resources in this article provide a point of departure for teachers and students to begin to appreciate this unique country that has added so much to the cultural wealth and prestige of the French-speaking world.

References

Adam, J. (2007, July). *Les particularismes historiques et institutionnels de la Belgique*. Lecture presented at the University of Mons-Hainaut, Mons, Belgium.

Belgian Railroad Web site. Retrieved on December 17, 2007, from http://www.b-rail.be/main/F/

Belgian Tourist Office. (2005). Retrieved on December 17, 2007, from http://www.visitbelgium.com/

Caesar, J. (1952). *Commentaries of Caesar on the Gallic War. Interlinear translation of the first seven books*. New York: David McKay.

Connais-tu la Belgique? (n.d.). Retrieved on December 17, 2007, from http://www.belgique.learningtogether.net/

Cook, B. A. (2002). *Belgium: A history*. New York: Lang.

Crousse, N. (2007). *Le Complexe belge: Petite psychanalyse d'un apatride*. Paris: Anabet.

Culture briefing: Belgium. Your guide to the culture and customs of the Belgian people. (2007). Kissimmee, FL: Geotravel Research Center.

Dubrulle, B. (2007). *Le petit futé Wallonie 2008*. Brussels: les Nouvelles Editions de l'Université.

L'État belge: Petite histoire de la Belgique et ses conséquences linguistiques. (2007).Retrieved on December 17, 2007, from the Université Laval Web site, http://www.tlfq.ulaval.ca/AXL/Europe/belgiqueetat_histoire.htm

Géographie. Retrieved on December 17, 2007, from the Portail fédéral de Belgique Web site: http://www.belgium.be/eportal/index.jsp

Gerard, J. (2005). How it all started is a mystery. Retrieved December 17, 2007, from http://www.belgianfries.com/

Le Guide des connaisseurs. (2004). L'Origine de la frite. Retrieved on December 17, 2007, from http://www.leguidedesconnaisseurs.be/article662.html

Heylighen, F. (1998). Belgium: Society, character and culture. An essay on the Belgian identity. In F. Heylighen, C. Joslyn, & V. Turchin (Eds.), *Principia Cybernetica Web*. Brussels: Principia Cybernetica. Retrieved on December 17, 2007, from http://pespmc1.vub.ac.be/BELGCUL2.html

Histoire. Retrieved on December 17, 2007, from the Portail fédéral de Belgique Web site: http://www.belgium.be/eportal/index.jsp

Histoire de la Belgique. Retrieved December 17, 2007, from the L'Internaute Web site: http://www.linternaute.com/histoire/histoire-de-la-belgique/belgique.shtml

Huggett, F. E. (1969). *Modern Belgium*. New York: Praeger.

Jackson, M. (2007). *Michael Jackson's great beers of Belgium*. Tielt, Belgium: Lannoo International.

Lange, D. L. (1998). The teaching of culture in foreign language courses. G. S. Burkart (Ed.), *Modules for the professional preparation of teaching assistants in foreign languages*. Washington, DC: Center for Applied Linguistics (ERIC Document No. ED433716)

Lebouc, G. (2006). *Dictionnaire de belgicismes*. Brussels: Racine.

Massion, F. (1987). *Dictionnaire de belgicismes*. 2 volumes. Frankfurt: Peter Lang.

National Standards in Foreign Language Education Project. (1999). *Standards for foreign language learning in the 21st century*. Yonkers, NY: Author.

Original Belgian Fries Web site. (2007). Retrieved December 17, 2007, from http://www.belgianfries.com/

Le petit futé Wallonie 2008 Web site. (2007). Retrieved December 17, 2007, from http://www.petitfute.be

Radio Télévision Belge de la Communauté Française. Retrieved December 17, 2007, from http://www.la1.be/index.htm

Tisseron, S. (2002). Family secrets and social memory in *Les aventures de Tintin*. *Yale French Studies,* No. 102 [*Belgian Memories*], 145-159.
Tutoweb.com (2004). Belgicismes. Retrieved on December 17, 2007, from http://www.tutoweb.com/belgicismes.htm

Appendix A: Sample Pre- and Post-test

(If the students' level of French does not allow the administration of this test in French, it can easily be translated into English.)

A la découverte de la Belgique:
1. Type du gouvernement:
2. Nom du souverain:
3. Drapeau (couleurs):
4. Hymne nationale:
5. Fête nationale:
6. Monnaie:
7. Langue(s) nationale(s):
8. Superficie:
9. Quelques grandes villes:
10. Pays limitrophes:
11. Nombre d'habitants:
12. Nom des habitants:
13. Monument(s) célèbre(s):
14. Personnages / personnalités célèbres:
15. Spécialités culinaires:

Appendix B: A Few Belgicisms and Their Equivalents in French and in American English

Belgicism	French	American English Equivalent of the Belgicism
baptême	bizutage	hazing
brosser un cours	sécher un cours	to skip class
carrousel	manège (forain)	carousel
chicon	endive	endive
copion	antisèche	cheat sheet
cramique	pain aux raisins secs	raisin roll
déjeuner	petit déjeuner	breakfast
dîner	déjeuner	lunch
divan	canapé	sofa
drache	forte averse	steady downfall
filet américain	steak tartare	steak tartare
GSM	téléphone portable	mobile phone
jatte	tasse	cup

jobiste	étudiant ayant un job	student worker
kot	chambre d'étudiant	room rented to a student
un matin	ce matin	this morning
mitraillette	steak haché frites	meat and *frites* sandwich
nonante	quatre-vingt-dix	ninety
octante	quatre-vingts	eighty
pistolet	un petit pain rond	a type of breakfast roll
praline	bouchée de chocolat	piece of chocolate
septante	soixante-dix	seventy
sonner	téléphoner	to call on the phone
souper	dîner /souper (familiar)	supper
torchon	serpillière	floor cloth
tute	sucette, tétine	pacifier
vidange	vidange (oil change)	bottle deposit

Appendix C: A Few Famous Belgians

Georges Simenon	Crime-fiction writer
Victor Horta	Art Nouveau architect
Georges Rémi (Hergé)	Creator of Tintin
Justine Henin	Tennis champion from Wallonia (Another tennis great is Kim Clijsters from Flanders.)
Eddy/Axel Merckx	Winner of the Tour de France five times; his son is also a cyclist.
Lara Fabian	Pop singer/songwriter
Jacques Brel	French-speaking singer, composer
Maurice Carême	Children's poet born in Wavre
Pierre Culliford (Peyo)	Creator of the Smurfs
The Brothers Dardenne	Film directors and two-time winners of the Palme d'Or at the Cannes Film Festival
Jean-Michel Folon	Artist, illustrator, painter, and sculptor born in Brussels
Philippe Geluck	Creator of the comic strip, "The Cat"
Maurice Grévisse	Famous grammarian, known for his *Le Bon Usage*
Audrey Hepburn	Actress
Claude Lévi-Strauss	Structural anthropologist born in Brussels in 1908
Maurice Maeterlinck	Poet, playwright, and essayist born in Ghent; awarded the Nobel Prize for Literature in 1911
René Magritte	Surrealist painter
Françoise Mallet-Joris	Writer, born in Anvers, elected one of 10 members of the Académie Goncourt
Henri Michaux	Poet, writer, and painter

Amélie Nothomb	Writer born in Japan to Belgian diplomats; published her first novel in 1992 and has been producing almost a novel a year since.
Axelle Red	Pop singer/songwriter
Jean-Claude Van Damme	Action-movie actor, known as the "Muscles from Brussels"
Adolphe Sax	Inventor of the saxophone in 1830

Appendix D: A Short List of Belgian Comic Strips and their Creators

Bob and Bobette	Willy Vandersteen
Boule and Bill	Jean Roba
The Cat (le Chat)	Philippe Geluck
Les Cités Obscures	François Schulten (artist) and Benoit Peeters (author)
Gaston Lagaffe	André Franquin
Lucky Luke	Created by Morris, who died in 2001; now written by René Goscinny
The Marsupilami	André Franquin (Disney adapted this comic strip into a cartoon.)
Les Schtroumpfs	Pierre Culliford
Tintin	Georges Rémi (Hergé)

Appendix E: A Day-Trip from Brussels

You are a tour director for Voyage Belgique Travel Agency, and you have been given a special assignment: You have the opportunity to lead a small group of students and their professor on a visit to French-speaking Belgium. Specifically, you will design a one-day excursion to the city of your choice from Brussels.

The tour program you design must include the following:

(1) Since the group will fly into Brussels, how does the group get to your city? Take a train? Take a bus? Where in your city will the selected mode of transportation drop off the group? Be sure to provide information about your return to Brussels.
(2) What are the places of cultural interest in the city? Make up a list of places to visit. Include two that are "must-see" places; two that would be good places to check out if there is enough time; two "might-be-interesting" places; and any other sights that you think are worth seeing. Remember that you have only one day in your city. You must tell why each of these places is worth visiting.

(3) Where is the group going to eat? Select two restaurant, one cheap and one expensive. Do NOT include McDonald's, Pizza Hut, or any other American restaurant. You must also tell what the group is going to eat; so describe any local specialties.
(4) What other special activities are available? What about shopping? What special events, such as local festivals and holiday events are unique to your city?

Present your program in a PowerPoint or poster presentation that includes all of the above information.

Because this is an academically-oriented trip, include also a one-paragraph description to introduce your city. In this paragraph, briefly describe its history. Then mention what makes the city important today. You may include references to industry, agriculture, government, tourism, or culture. Be sure to include information on climate and population.

Include with your paragraph an outline map of Belgium. Shade in the province in which your city is located, mark the city's location with a star, and label them both.

(Note: This project may be done in French or in English.)

Southern Conference on Language Teaching
Board of Directors
2007-2008

Norah Jones [2008]
President

Vista Higher Learning
National Consultant, Gladys, VA

Marsha Johnson [2008]
Conference Program Director

Lexington High School
Lexington, SC

Lynn Fulton-Archer [2009]
President Elect/Advocacy Director

Richmond Drive Elementary School
Rock Hill, SC

Ken Stewart [2009]
Teacher of the Year Awards Director

Chapel Hill High School
Chapel Hill, NC

Jacki Cinotti-Dirmann [2010]
Awards and Program Co-Director

Ocean Way Middle School
Jacksonville, FL

Nancy Decker [2010]
Scholarship Director

Rollins College
Winter Park, FL

Patricia Carlin [2011]
SCOLTalk Editor

University of Central Arkansas
Conway, AR

Kenneth Gordon [2011]
Electronic Media Director

Winthrop College
Rock Hill, SC

Jim Chesnut
Past President

North Georgia College and State
University Dahlonega, GA

Maurice Cherry
Dimension Co-Editor
SCOLT Representative to ACTFL

Furman University
Greenville, SC

Carol Wilkerson
Dimension Co-Editor

Western Kentucky University
Bowling Green, KY

Carolyn L. Hansen
Dimension Publisher

University of South Carolina
Columbia, SC

Lynne McClendon, ✣
Executive Director

Retired Consultant
Roswell, GA

✣ **ordre des palmes académiques**

SCOLT
Southern Conference on Language Teaching

2007 Individual Sponsors

Marty Abbott	VA	Luana Coleman	SC
Phyllis Yewell Adams	VA	Michel Couet	SC
Polly Adkins	SC	Judith Cox	AL
David Alley	GA	Tamara Cox	NC
Maria Arnett	GA	Joanna Crane	AL
Jason Bagley	SC	Kristin Crews	TN
Greg Barfield	GA	Adanise Cruz	FL
Sue Barry	AL	Rhonda Daniels	AR
John Bartley	GA	Nancy Decker	FL
Laura Beasley	TN	Monica De Rivera	FL
Mary Ellen Beaton	VA	Antonio Diaz	NC
Lounell Beecher	GA	Jeri Dies	GA
Jenn Bonn	GA	Clarice Doucette	TN
Herman Bostick	MD	Chantal Dulieu	FL
Jody Boyd	SC	Sandy DuVall	GA
Peggy Boyles	OK	Daphne Eidson	GA
Lee Bradley	GA	Lollie Eykyn	SC
Evelyn Brady	GA	Leila Falt	AL
Kathy Brantley	GA	Diana Ferreira	GA
Maureen Browne	FL	Anna Maria Ford	SC
Paul Bryant	TN	Lisa Foster	VA
Anita Burke-Morton	GA	Teresa Franson	VA
Michael Burriss	AL	Lynn Fulton-Archer	SC
Beatriz Bustillo	FL	Michelle Fulwider	NC
Donna Butler	AL	Howard Furnas	AL
Susan Campbell	SC	Tammy Garces	GA
Lilia Cano	GA	Alicia Gimenez	AL
Patricia Carlin	AR	Ransom Gladwin	GA
Jean Paul Carton	GA	Monique Glover	GA
Doreen Cestari	GA	Farley Gordon	SC
Mirella Chavez	AL	Kenneth Gordon	SC
Rosalie Cheatham	AR	John Green	GA
Ginette Chenard	GA	Marcia Grimes	GA
Sharon Cherry	SC	Cecilia Guerrero	GA
Jim Chesnut	GA	Paula Heusinkveld	SC
Jacki Cinotti-Dirmann	FL	Mirella J. Hodges	AL
Nancy Ciudad-Simons	GA	Mary Jim Howe	SC

Louise Ann Hunley	FL	Silvia Pulido	FL
Shirley Hurd	GA	Gloria Quave	SC
Catherine Hutchinson	TN	Kim Rampley	GA
David Jahner	GA	Matt Ramsby	SC
Marsha Johnson	SC	Sharon Rapp	AR
Myra Johnson	FL	Melyn Roberson	GA
Gale Jones	FL	Margaret Roberts	SC
Norah Jones	VA	Cathy Robison	SC
Glenna Kappel	FL	Tracy Rucker	GA
Tammy Kasserman	NC	Tamara Salgado	FL
Jacqueline Konan	GA	Marat Sanatullov	KS
Jean Koehler	NC	Elvira Sanatullova-Allison	NY
Richard LaFleur	GA	Sylvia Sandin	FL
Lizette Mujica Laughlin	SC	Monika Santiago	SC
Douglas Lightfoot	AL	Esperanza Sasser	GA
Sheri Long	AL	Virginia Scott	TN
Maria Lopez	GA	Lisa Signori	SC
Ines Lormand	TX	Maggie Smallwood	NC
Linda Maier	AL	Robin Snyder	WV
Linda Markley	FL	Samia Spencer	AL
Judith Martin	FL	Edwina Spodark	VA
Gudrun Martyny	FL	Jonita Stepp-Greany	FL
Elaine McAllister	GA	Ken Stewart	NC
Lynne McClendon	GA	Alice Strange	MO
Sheilia McCoy	GA	Colleen Tavares	GA
Mary McGehee	LA	Robert Terry	VA
Susan McLeish	GA	Elizabeth Thompson	NC
Jorge Medina	SC	Nellie Tietz	AL
Frank Medley	SC	Deborah Tucker	TN
Anna Megyesi	WV	Linda Villadoniga	FL
Linda Meigs	AL	Alyssa Villarrea	TN
Carlos Mentley	SC	Joan Viteri	NC
Dana Miller	GA	Hilary Wagner	GA
Dennis Miller, Jr.	GA	Brenda Watkins	GA
Juan Carlos Morales	FL	Carol Wilkerson	KY
Charles Moore	NC	Debbie Williams	AL
Joann Mount	NC	Sarah Williams	SC
Susan Neese	TN	John Williams III	GA
Hannah Nershi	LA	John Wilson	GA
Pat Nix	AL	David Witkosky	AL
Denise Overfield	GA	Ava Wyatt	GA
Linda Paragone	AL	Katherine Young	SC
Osvaldo Parrilla	SC	Mary Yudin	FL
Edwin Perez	GA		
Kristen Perez	GA		

2007 SCOLT Patrons Representing Institutions and Organizations

American Association of Teachers of German (AATG)
   Helene Zimmer-Loew, Executive Director
American Council on the Teaching of Foreign Languages (ACTFL)
   Bret Lovejoy , Executive Director, and **Ray Clifford, President**
Arkansas Department of Education (Little Rock, AR)
   Ellen E. Treadway, Language Consultant
Augusta State University (Augusta, GA)
   Jana Sandarg and **Robert Flannigan**
Brevard Public Schools (FL)
   Tracy Veler Knick
Boca Beth, Inc. (Tampa, FL)
   Beth Butler
Cemanahuac Ed. Community (Mexico)
   Vivian Harvey
Central States Conference on Language Teaching (CSC)
   Patrick Raven, Executive Director
Centro Mundo Lengua (Spain)
   David Hirsch
Chattanooga School for Arts and Sciences, CSAS (Chattanooga, TN)
   Daniel Morgan
Consulat Général de France d'Atlanta & the Cultural Services of the French Embassy (Atlanta, GA)
   Diane Josse and **Julie Fournier-Angelo**
Covenant Day School (Matthews, NC)
   Caroline Switzer Kelly
Cumming Elementary School (Cumming, GA)
   Karenina Campos and **Claudia Juliana Cruz**
Embassy of Spain, Ministry of Education and Science (Atlanta, GA)
   Eva Martínez, Education Advisor
Estudio Sampere (Spain)
   Juan Manuel Sampere
Florida Chapter of the American Association of Teachers of French
   Deanna Scheffer
Furman University (Greenville, SC)
   Maurice Cherry

Georgia Department of Education (Atlanta, GA)
    Susan Crooks, Language Consultant; Wayne Craven, ESOL; Carol Johnson, ESOL; Chris Scott, ESOL; Mae Lombos Wlazlinski, ESOL; and **Elizabeth Webb, Innovative Programs**
Georgia Southern University (Statesboro, GA)
    Clara Krug and **Horst Kurz**
InterPrep, Inc. (Marietta, GA)
    Greg Duncan
Kennesaw State University (Kennesaw, GA)
    Rosa Bobia
Kentucky Department of Education (Frankfort, KY)
    Jacque Bott Van Houten, Language Consultant
Lakeside High School (Evans, GA)
    Angelica Eubanks
Louisiana Department of Education (Baton Rouge, LA)
    Terri Hammatt, Language Consultant
Macon State College (Macon, GA)
    Lynn Byrant and **David de Posada**
Mississippi Gulf Coast Community College (Gulfport, MS)
    Vernon LaCour
Mississippi Department of Education (Jackson, MS)
    Rhonda Smith, Language Consultant
National FLES Institute (Rockville, MD)
    Gladys Lipton, Executive Director
National Spanish Examinations (Valparaiso, IN)
    Kevin Cessna-Buscemi
North Carolina Department of Public Istruction (Raleigh, NC)
    Ann Marie Gunter, Language Consultant, and **Helga Fasciano, Section Chief, K-12 Programs**
North Carolina State University (Raleigh, NC)
    Susan Navey-Davis
North Georgia College and State University (Dahlonega, GA)
    Elizabeth Combier
Northeast Conference on the Teaching of Foreign Languages (NECTFL)
    Rebecca Kline
Pacific Northwest Council for Languages (PNCFL)
    Greg Hooper-Moore
Pearson, Prentice Hall
    Lucy Amarillo
Pine Crest School (Ft. Lauderdale, FL)
    Frank J. Kruger-Robbins
Randolph School (Huntsville, AL)
    Peggy Bilbro
SCOLA (McClelland, IA)
    Leslie Parker Bryant

South Carolina Department of Education (Columbia, SC)
    Ruta Couet, Language Consultant
South Carolina Foreign Language Teachers' Association (SCFLTA)
    Shawn Morrison and **Diane Schiferl**
Southwest Conference on Language Teaching (SWCOLT)
    Jody Klopp
Spalding High School (Griffin, GA)
    Todd Benz
St. Martin Parish Schools (St. Martinsville, LA)
    Peggy Feehan
Tennessee Chapter of the American Association of Teachers of Spanish and Portuguese
    Deb Lamine and **Dorothy Winkles**
Tougaloo College (Tougaloo, MS)
    Mary Davis
Université du Quebec à Chicoutimi (Canada)
    Pierre Lincourt
University of Central Florida (Orlando, FL)
    Karen Verkler
University of South Carolina (Columbia, SC)
    Lara Ducate and **Carolyn L. Hansen**
Valdosta State University (Valdosta, GA)
    Ellen Friedrich and **Vicki Soady**
Virginia Department of Education (Richmond, VA)
    Helen Small
Virgin Islands Department of Education
    Myrna V. van Beverhoudt
Walker School (Marietta, GA)
    Maria Croley and **Jane Spears**
West Virginia Department of Education (Charleston, WV)
    Robert Crawford, Language Consultant
West Virginia Foreign Language Teachers' Association (WVFLTA)
    David Marlow, Executive Director, and **Terri Marlow, Treasurer**

Previous Editions of SCOLT's *Dimension* Available for Purchase

From Practice to Profession: Dimension 2007

Jacque Bott Van Houten	NCSSFL's LinguaFolio Project
Carolyn Gascoigne	Misperceptions of Attitudes Toward Language Study
Nike Arnold	Student Perspectives on Foundation Issues in Articulation
Catherine T. Johnson	Germany's Multicultural and Multiracial Issues
Patricia Thomas	Representation of Latino Culture in Introductory High School Textbooks
Anne Fountain and Catherine Fountain	Maya and Nahuatl in the Teaching of Spanish: Expanding the Professional Perspective
Rosalie M. Cheatham	A 21st Century Approach to Integrating Culture and Communication
Marat Sanatullov and Elvira Sanatullova-Allison	Integrating Stories with Multimedia into the French Language Classroom

Languages for Today's World: Dimension 2006

Marcia L. Wilbur	Engaging Students in the L2 Reading Process
Jean LeLoup and Robert Ponterio	FLTEACH Project: Online Database of Model Lessons with Cultural Content
Zachary Jones and Bernice Nuhfer-Halten	Use of Blogs in L2 Instruction
Kenneth A. Gordon	Developing a Contemporary French Civilization Course: An Annotated Review of Internet Resources
Steven M. Gardner, Carlos Mentley, and Lisa F. Signori	The Roads to Compostela: An Immersion Experience in Germany, France, and Spain
Paula Heusinkveld	Talking About Music: Ethnographic Interviews on Traditional Hispanic Songs

Rebecca Burns-Hoffman, Jennifer Jones, and Christie Cohn — Teaching and Learning American Sign Language in U. S. Schools

Languages and Language Learners: Dimension 2005

Krista S. Chambless — Effects of FLEX Programs on Elementary Students' Attitudes Towards Foreign Languages and Cultures

Marian M. Brodman — Developing Vocabulary Beyond the Word

Robert M. Terry — The Reading Process: Realistic Expectations for Reading in Lower-Level Language Classes

Carmen Schlig — Improving Foreign Language Writing Competence

David C. Alley — Using Computer Translation Websites to Further the Objectives of the Foreign Language Standards

Karen Verkler — Rebuilding a Dying Foreign Language Education Program

Darrell J. Dernoshek and Lara C. Ducate — Graduate Teaching Assistant Training: Pathways to Success

Carol Wilkerson; with Sue Barry, Gladys Lipton, Carol Semonsky, and Sheri Spaine Long — Assessment and Assessment Design 1994-2004: An Annotated Bibliography

Assessment Practices in Foreign Language Education: Dimension 2004

Lynne McClendon — No Child Left Behind in Foreign Language Education

Rosalie M. Cheatham — Using Learner and Teacher Preparation Standards to Reform a Language Major

Denise Egéa-Kuehne — Student Electronic Portfolio Assessment

Carol Wilkerson, Judith H. Schomber, and Jana Sandarg — Assessing Readiness of FL Education Majors to Take the Praxis II Exam

Scott Grubbs — The TPR Test: Total Physical Response as an Assessment Tool

Victoria Rodrigo — Assessing the Impact of Narrow Listening: Students' Perceptions and Performance

Miguel Montero	Accounting for Activity: Cognition and Oral Proficiency Assessment
Sharron Gray Abernethy	Building Bridges for International Internships

Models for Excellence in Second Language Education: Dimension 2003

Lourdes Sánchez-López and Jessica Ramos-Harthun	The Transnational Classroom: Connecting People, Languages, and Cultures
Denise M. Overfield	Creating a Language Learning Community Within and Beyond the Classroom
Betina Kaplan and Teresa Pérez-Gamboa	Stepping Out of the Classroom to Increase Spanish Language Skills and Cultural Awareness
Lara Lomicka, Gillian Lord, and Melanie Manzerin	Merging Foreign Language Theory and Practice: Designing Technology-Based Tasks
Janet Flewelling	Creating Narrated Multimedia Presentations in the Second and Foreign Language Class
Carmen Chaves Tesser and Marty Abbott	INTASC Model Foreign Language Standards for Beginning Teacher Licensing and Development
Anja Bernardy and Elaine McAllister	Alternative Teacher Preparation Programs in Foreign Languages
Sue Barry	Group Study Abroad and Thematic Units

Cyberspace and Foreign Languages: Making the Connection: Dimension 2002

Darrell J. Dernoshek and Lara L. Lomicka	Connecting Through Cyberspace: Correspondence Projects for Beginning and Intermediate Students
Carmen Villegas Rogers	Tradition &Technology in Language Teaching
Janet Flewelling	From Language Lab to Multimedia Lab: Oral Language Assessment
Hye-Yeon Lim and W. I. Griffith	Idiom Instruction Through Multimedia and Cultural Concepts
Antje Krueger	Online Writing and Reading: Powerful Communicative Tools for L2 Acquisition
María J. Amores	Contextualizing Culture: Using Authentic Resources to Develop Cultural Awareness

Karen Elkins and Robin Boulton	Project-Based Learning in the Foreign Language Classroom
Claudia Smith Salcedo and Lucia Guzzi Harrison	The Effect of Songs on Text Recall and Involuntary Mental Rehearsal in Foreign Language Learning
Jacque Bott Van Houten	Teacher Academies: Professional Development for a Community of Learners

The Odyssey Continues: Dimension 2001

T. Bruce Fryer	Four Decades of Foreign Language Education: Are We Still at Cheese Station N?
Jean-Louis P. Dassier	Teaching Students with the Internet: What the Students Want vs. What They Do
Laura Semones and Rebecca Chism	Learning Behind the Screen: Computers, Conversations, Communities
James C. Davidheiser	The ABC's of Total Physical Response Storytelling
Paula Heusinkveld	Understanding Hispanic Culture Through Music: The Theme of Nostalgia
Francis Achampong and Enrique G. Zapatero	Enhancing the Study of International Business, Foreign Languages, and the Nonlanguage Aspects of Intercultural Communication
Jean-Louis P. Dassier and William Powell	Formative Foreign Language Program Evaluation

New Millennium, New Directions: Dimension 2000

Heide R. Lomangino	A Systematic Approach to Second Language Vocabulary Instruction
Elizabeth G. Joiner	Listening Training for Language Learners: The Tomatis Approach to Second Language Acquisition
Virginia M. Scott and Lara E. Semones	Thinking Together: Student Interaction During the FL Writing Process
James C. Davidheiser	The European Union and the Second Language Curriculum of the 21st Century
Jayne Abrate	Making Cultural Learning Authentic: Going Beyond Stereotype and Anecdote

David W. Seaman	Correcting the Problem of Freeze-Frame Cultural Stereotyping: Case Study–Martinique
Carolyn Gascoigne Lally	Extramural Standards: Foreign Language Learning Beyond the Classroom
Jean-Louis P. Dassier and Lee Wilberschied	A Case Study of Reflection in Supervision: Does It Have Any Relationship to Interns' Reflectivity?

Volumes for 2005, 2006, 2007, and 2008 are available for purchase at $10 each. Previous volumes of *Dimension* are available for purchase at $5.00 each.

EIN 23-7027288

Lynne McClendon
SCOLT Executive Director
165 Lazy Laurel Chase
Roswell, GA 30076-3677

Telephone 770-992-1256   http://www.scolt./org
Fax 770-992-3464   lynnemcc@mindspring.com